Pillsbury Bake-Off®

prize-winning recipes

100 Top Recipes from the
43rd Pillsbury Bake-Off® Contest

WILEY

Wiley Publishing, Inc.

For general information on our other products and services or for technical support, please contact our Customer Care Department within the United States at (877) 762-2974, outside the United States at (317) 572-3993 or fax (317) 572-4002.

Wiley also publishes its books in a variety of electronic formats. Some content that appears in print may not be available in electronic books. For more information about Wiley products, visit our Web site at www.wiley.com.

LIBRARY OF CONGRESS CATALOGING-IN-PUBLICATION DATA:

Pillsbury bake-off prize-winning recipes : 100 top recipes from the 43rd Pillsbury Bake-Off Contest.

    p. cm.

Includes index.

ISBN 978-0-470-39703-9 (pbk.)

1. Baking. 2. Quick and easy cookery. I. Pillsbury Company II. Bake-Off (Contest)

TX765.P519273 2009

641.8'15--dc22

              2008038582

Printed in China

10 9 8 7 6 5 4 3 2 1

Cover photo: "Peanut Butter-licious" Ring-a-Rounds, page 12

GENERAL MILLS

Editorial Director: **Jeff Nowak**

Manager and Editor, Cookbooks: **Lois Tlusty**

Recipe Testing: **Pillsbury Test Kitchens**

Photography: **General Mills Studios and Image Library**

Photographers: **Val Bourassa and Andy Swarbrick**

Food Stylists: **Nancy Johnson, Sharon Harding, Sue Brue and Cindy Syme**

WILEY PUBLISHING, INC.

Publisher: **Natalie Chapman**

Executive Editor: **Anne Ficklen**

Senior Editorial Assistant: **Charleen Barila**

Senior Production Editor: **Amy Zarkos**

Cover Design: **Suzanne Sunwoo**

Art Director: **Tai Blanche**

Interior Design: **Holly Wittenberg**

Interior Layout: **Indianapolis Composition Services**

Manufacturing Manager: **Kevin Watt**

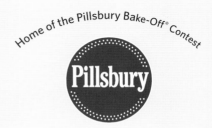

Home of the Pillsbury Bake-Off® Contest

Our recipes have been tested in the Pillsbury Kitchens and meet our standards of easy preparation, reliability and great taste.

For more great recipes visit pillsbury.com

Dear Friends,

You can imagine how excited we are to receive the tens of thousands of entries for the Pillsbury Bake-Off® Contest. We can't wait to see all the new ideas! We are always very impressed by the creativity of America's home cooks.

From the 43rd Pillsbury Bake-Off® Contest entries, we determined that today's cooks are ingredient savvy and know how to balance flavors and textures. These cooks also know how to use their skills—and time—to get the "wow factor" in foods. For example, they created high-flavor fillings and toppings. And rather than add a garnish, they simply built extra touches into their recipes.

For the Bake-Off® Kitchens, it was no small task to determine the best recipes for the competition. We used rigorous screening, taste panels and kitchen testing to select the top 100 recipes.

On April 14, 2008, the amateur cooks who created these winning recipes gathered at The Fairmont Hotel & Resort in Dallas, Texas, to participate in the 43rd Pillsbury Bake-Off® Contest finals.

While only one recipe can win the $1 million Grand Prize, the other 99 finalists can be assured that their recipe creations are among America's best. We hope you enjoy this collection of 100 great recipes and trust that they will soon become some of your family's favorites.

Sincerely,

Jann Atkins

Jann Atkins
Bake-Off® Kitchens Manager
43rd Pillsbury Bake-Off® Contest

contents

Grand Prize $1 Million Winner:
DOUBLE-DELIGHT PEANUT BUTTER COOKIES (p. 186)
Carolyn Gurtz, Gaithersburg, Maryland

Pillsbury Bake-Off® Contest
memories and recipes

The first Pillsbury Bake-Off® Contest was created to bring forth treasured recipes from around the country and honor America's best cooks. It was 1949 and World War II, with its food shortages and ration stamps, was history. The post-war economy was thriving and people had time and money again to enjoy good food and entertaining.

Originally called the Grand National Recipe and Baking Contest, the first contest was so popular it was repeated the next year. The contest was held annually until 1976 and then changed to an every-other-year schedule. Now, nearly 60 years later, the contest remains popular as it continues to reflect the changing food needs and interests.

award-winning recipes from the 43rd Pillsbury Bake-Off® Contest

The 100 recipes in this cookbook were created by amateur cooks who share a passion for creativity in the kitchen, just like the thousands of Bake-Off® Contest finalists before them. Each of the finalists in the 43rd Bake-Off® Contest perfected an innovative new recipe idea that combines great taste and appearance with overall appeal that's sure to make these family favorites.

create your own memories

Throughout this cookbook you'll find a variety of recipes to make for your family and friends, whether it's a weeknight meal, a holiday dinner or a casual weekend get-together. Each time you prepare a recipe, jot down a notation about when you served it and the occasion, and this cookbook will become a family keepsake.

competing in the 43rd Pillsbury Bake-Off® Contest

The Pillsbury Bake-Off® Contest has stayed much the same since the very first contest. One hundred mini kitchens are set up at the Fairmont Hotel & Resort in Dallas, Texas. On competition day, finalists prepare

fun fact The first contest was held in 1949 at New York City's Waldorf-Astoria Hotel. Prizes were presented by Art Linkletter and Eleanor Roosevelt. One of three male finalists in that contest, T. O. Davis, wrote: "Mrs. Roosevelt was a doll. Everyone loved her charm and candor. 'I am very fond of good cooking,' she said, 'but I'm afraid I'm a very poor cook.'"

their recipes and a panel of judges tastes and reviews the recipes. The judging criteria for the 43rd Pillsbury Bake-Off® Contest are taste, appearance, creativity and consumer appeal.

stocking the mini kitchens

Weeks before the contest, a Bake-Off® assistant manager reads the 100 winning recipes and visualizes what kitchen equipment is needed to prepare each recipe from start to finish. She then compiles individual equipment lists for each finalist to review. After the lists have been approved, the equipment is pulled from the Bake-Off® warehouse and a box is packed and labeled for each finalist's mini kitchen. Once the cabinets and ranges are in place, the Bake-Off® team goes to work filling the cupboards.

the 100 finalists

Finalists in the 43rd Pillsbury Bake-Off® Contest gather on the edge of the official contest floor, where the talented home cooks from 35 different states will compete for the $1 million Grand Prize. Turn to p. 224 for the names and home states of all 100 finalists.

fun fact Finalists submit their grocery lists and a master list is compiled, consisting of all the food items needed to prepare each recipe three times. Fresh produce on the 43rd Bake-Off® Contest grocery list included: 67 onions, 45 bunches of bananas, 45 limes, 43 tomatoes, 38 jalapeño chiles, 34 avocados, 32 bunches of cilantro, 23 oranges, 20 bunches of green onions, 18 poblano chiles, 15 garlic bulbs and 11 bunches of basil.

fun facts

- Eight finalists are men.
- Ages range from 27 to 72.
- California has the most finalists; seven didn't leave Texas to compete and one finalist, from Kodiak Island, Alaska, traveled the farthest.
- Finalists' careers vary from air traffic controller to gemologist, software developer to mechanical engineer. Twenty finalists are stay-at-home moms.
- Twenty-two of the finalists are professional musicians or listed music as a hobby or passion. One is a full-time pianist, one plays in a rock band and another is a singer/songwriter who has recorded her own CD.

fun fact About one month before the Pillsbury Bake-Off® Contest, finalists receive a letter with travel information and suggestions about what to pack. In the 1949 letter, Ann Pillsbury wrote: "You might bring a housedress of some kind that you like to cook in, but you won't need an apron because Pillsbury will furnish all the contestants with aprons they may keep for souvenirs." The apron for the 43rd contest was designed with the Dallas location in mind. The dark brown apron features khaki-colored Western accent stitching and a blue jeans–style pocket.

7:50 a.m. *Finalists Make the Grand March*

The contest day starts with breakfast and remarks at 6:15 a.m. At 7:20, finalists don their aprons and line up for the Grand March onto the contest floor. Gretchen Wanek, Oshkosh, Wisconsin, assigned to Range 1, and Jasmine Buliga, Braintree, Massachusetts, Range 100, lead the procession.

8 a.m. *Let the Contest Begin*

An official announcement is made that the contest will now start. Finalists take the supplies out of the cabinets as the competition begins. Only finalists and authorized assistants are allowed on the contest floor for the first 20 minutes.

8:59 a.m. *The First Recipe Is Submitted*

Margaret Blount, Morehead City, North Carolina, submits her Sweet-and-Sour Shrimp Puffs recipe (p. 86) for judging.

11 a.m. *Most Finalists Are Still Cooking*

When a finalist is ready to bring his or her entry to the judges' room, a Bake-Off® Contest assistant clears a path through the crowd by calling out, "Recipe coming through!"

12:54 p.m. *The Last Recipe Is Submitted*

Just six minutes before the contest officially ends, Jane Estrin, Gainesville, Florida, submits her recipe, Pistachio Mousse Brownie Torte (p. 208). The nine judges, a panel of food experts, will finish tasting the recipes and then face the difficult task of choosing the Grand Prize Winner.

1 p.m. *Contest Officially Ends*

Within minutes of the contest ending, dismantling of the competition floor begins to transform the ballroom to the setting for the next morning's awards ceremony.

7 p.m. *Time to Relax*

The finalists kick back and relax at a Texas-themed dinner and party, featuring great food, a live country-western band and dancing. Even the Pillsbury Doughboy™ did a little line dancing!

Next morning, 8 a.m. *And the Winners Are . . .*

The 100 finalists and guests are seated at the Awards Ceremony, anxiously awaiting the announcement of the prize winners, including the 43rd Bake-Off® Contest Grand Prize Winner. Who will be America's new Bake-Off® millionaire?

meet the $1 million winner

Carolyn Gurtz, Gaithersburg, Maryland, is named the Grand Prize Winner for her Double-Delight Peanut Butter Cookies (p. 186). The contest judges agreed that Carolyn's recipe surpassed the 99 other competitors for its simplicity and approachability, allowing the home cook to take a convenience product and turn it into an unexpected cookie that bursts with layers of peanut butter flavor.

In an interview following the contest, Carolyn said, "Just being a finalist was such a thrill for me, and then to have won the grand prize, I'm just flabbergasted. And then I started thinking that my recipe will be published as a Grand Prize Winner for the Pillsbury Bake-Off® Contest. People will be making the cookie I created. I just can't believe it."

category and prize winners

Five finalists receive a $5,000 cash prize plus a brand new range for their winning recipe in each of five categories. In addition to the category winners, three special awards are given.

Breakfast & Brunches: Casual brunch or weekend family breakfast ideas, such as sweet rolls, breakfast breads or egg dishes. Pamela Shank, Parkersburg, West Virginia, won for her Mascarpone-Filled Cranberry-Walnut Rolls (p. 34).

Entertaining Appetizers: Appetizer and snack ideas to serve at casual gatherings with family and friends or for holiday entertaining. Edgar Rudberg, St. Paul, Minnesota, won for his Salmon Pastries with Dill Pesto (p. 78).

Old El Paso® Mexican Favorites: Tacos, burritos, enchiladas, fajitas, quesadillas or other dishes that creatively use Mexican-inspired flavors and an Old El Paso® product. Vanda Pozzanghera, Pittsford, New York, won for her Mexican Pesto-Pork Tacos (p. 112).

Pizza Creations: Snack or family pizzas, calzones, panini and more made with Pillsbury® Refrigerated Pizza Crust. Niki Plourde, Gardner, Massachusetts, won for her Apple-Jack Chicken Pizza with Caramelized Onions (p. 142).

Sweet Treats: Quick and easy treats for anytime celebrations, such as cookies, pies, tarts, brownies or bars. Carolyn Gurtz, Gaithersburg, Maryland, was the winner of this category, for her Double-Delight Peanut Butter Cookies (p. 186), and was also named the Grand Prize Winner.

America's Favorite Recipe Winner: Consumers voted online January through March 2008 for their favorite recipe. Gwen Beauchamp, Lancaster, Texas, won the $5,000 America's Favorite Recipe award. Her recipe for Toffee-Banana Brownies (p. 216) received the most consumer votes.

GE Imagination at Work Award: This award recognizes the most innovative recipe. Phyllis Weeks-Daniel, San Diego, California, won for her Blue Cheese and Red Onion Jam Crescent Thumbprints (p. 56). She received $5,000 in GE Profile™ kitchen appliances.

Jif® Peanut Butter Award: This award recognizes the best recipe using at least $1/4$ cup of Jif® Peanut Butter. Carolyn Gurtz, Gaithersburg, Maryland, also received this $5,000 award for her Double-Delight Peanut Butter Cookies (p. 186).

fun facts Finalists say that if they win the $1 million prize money they will:

- Pay off the mortgage.
- Save for their children's education or pay off their own student loans.
- Save for retirement or simply retire early.
- Take a dream trip to Egypt, France or Japan or a Baltic Sea cruise.
- Plant a pecan orchard.

Pamela Shank, Parkersburg, West Virginia, won $5,000 and a brand new range for her Mascarpone-Filled Cranberry-Walnut Rolls (p. 34). Pamela came up with her recipe idea when she was making a pull-apart bread with her granddaughter.

chapter one

breakfast & brunches

Treat family and friends to a casual brunch or one of these weekend breakfast ideas, such as sweet rolls, breakfast breads or egg dishes.

Trends in Breakfast & Brunch Category

Tropical fruits and flavors were popular, such as coconut, pineapple, papaya and mango.

Many recipes called for ramekins to create individual portions. Muffin pans were frequently used, from mini- to Texas-size cups.

Classic recipes were used in a new way, such as Reuben Quiche, Corn Chowder Quiche and Chicken Pot Pie Quiche. Variations of bread pudding were popular, too.

Liquor and liqueurs were common ingredients in many of the recipes as flavor enhancements. Recipes called for beer, white wine, apricot brandy, cherry brandy, whiskey, Kahlua®, Grand Marnier®, amaretto and rum. Coconut rum flavored a glaze and wine was used in an egg dish.

ROLLS

1/3 cup powdered sugar

1/4 cup creamy peanut butter

2 tablespoons butter or margarine, softened

1/2 teaspoon banana extract

2 cans (11 oz each) Pillsbury® refrigerated original breadsticks (12 breadsticks each)

GLAZE

1/2 cup milk chocolate chips

3 tablespoons butter or margarine

2 teaspoons light corn syrup

1/8 teaspoon vanilla

1/8 teaspoon banana extract

1/4 cup chopped pecans

Erika Couch | Frederick, MD

Erika Couch's creative pairing of breadsticks coiled around the flavors of chocolate, banana and peanut butter is a new "twist" on her usual baking specialties: chocolate cake and sweet rolls. Erika lived in East Germany behind the Iron Curtain as a child, "where life was not so good," she recalls. Later, she and her family managed to escape to West Germany. Erika says she spends most of her time in her kitchen, reading cookbooks or chatting with her daughter.

"peanut butter-licious" ring-a-rounds

12 rolls | Prep Time: **25 minutes** | Start to Finish: **50 minutes**

1 Heat oven to 375°F. Spray large cookie sheet with cooking spray. In small bowl, stir powdered sugar, peanut butter, 2 tablespoons butter and 1/2 teaspoon banana extract until smooth; set aside.

2 Unroll both cans of dough on cutting board; divide into 4 equal sections along center perforations. Spread about 1/4 cup peanut butter mixture over each of 2 dough sections. Place remaining dough sections over filling. Using sharp knife, cut along perforations into 12 strips. Gently stretch each strip until about 10 inches long. Twist each strip 4 or 5 times. Coil each strip into pinwheel shape; tuck end under. Place 2 inches apart on cookie sheet.

3 Bake 12 to 18 minutes or until golden brown. Remove rolls from cookie sheet to cooling rack placed on waxed paper. Cool 10 minutes.

4 Meanwhile, in 2-quart saucepan, melt chocolate chips, 3 tablespoons butter and the corn syrup over medium heat, stirring occasionally, until chocolate chips are melted and mixture is smooth. Stir in vanilla and 1/8 teaspoon banana extract.

5 Drizzle glaze over warm rolls. Sprinkle each with 1 teaspoon pecans. Serve warm or at room temperature.

High Altitude (3500–6500 ft): Heat oven to 350°F. Bake 14 to 20 minutes.

1 **Roll:** Calories 290; Total Fat 14g (Saturated Fat 6g; Trans Fat 0g); Cholesterol 15mg; Sodium 400mg; Total Carbohydrate 35g (Dietary Fiber 0g) **Exchanges:** 1 1/2 Starch, 1 Other Carbohydrate, 2 1/2 Fat **Carbohydrate Choices:** 2

CRUST

1 can (13.9 oz) Pillsbury refrigerated orange flavor sweet rolls with icing
2 tablespoons apricot preserves
$\frac{1}{4}$ cup sliced almonds

FILLING

2 packages (8 oz each) cream cheese, softened
Icing from can of sweet rolls
1 teaspoon vanilla
$\frac{1}{8}$ teaspoon salt
2 eggs

TOPPING

$\frac{1}{4}$ cup apricot preserves
$\frac{1}{4}$ cup sliced almonds

GARNISH, IF DESIRED

Fresh strawberries
Fresh mint leaves

Mary Beth Mandola | Houston, TX

Imagine a delicious orange-flavored tart with a delicate orange cheese-cake filling, sweet apricot swirls and toasted almonds. That's **Mary Beth Mandola**'s entry for an elegant brunch tart. Her recipe is ideal for a special occasion or family morning, she says. Mary Beth and her husband are of Italian descent, which she says accounts for lots of family, food and conversation in the kitchen. Her favorite family meal is dinner. "Everyone scatters during the day. Dinner is a good time to come together."

apricot-orange brunch tart

16 servings | Prep Time: **20 minutes** | Start to Finish: **2 hours 45 minutes**

1 Heat oven to 350°F. Spray 10-inch nonstick tart pan with removable bottom with cooking spray. Place orange rolls in bottom of pan, spacing evenly; press rolls together to cover bottom of pan. Set icing aside.

2 Brush 2 tablespoons preserves over rolls. Sprinkle $\frac{1}{4}$ cup almonds over rolls.

3 In large bowl, beat cream cheese, icing, vanilla and salt with electric mixer on medium speed until smooth. Beat in eggs, one at a time, scraping bowl occasionally, until smooth and creamy.

4 Gently spoon filling over almonds on rolls, spreading to edge of pan and smoothing top. Cut up large fruit pieces in $\frac{1}{4}$ cup preserves if necessary. Drop preserves in small spoonfuls randomly over filling. Swirl preserves into filling, using knife. Sprinkle $\frac{1}{4}$ cup almonds around edge of tart.

5 Place pan on cookie sheet. Bake 35 to 40 minutes or until edge is golden brown and filling is set. Cool in pan 15 minutes. Remove side of pan; place tart on serving plate.* Refrigerate uncovered 1 hour 30 minutes or until chilled.

6 To serve, cut tart into wedges, using sharp knife. Garnish serving plate with strawberries and mint leaves. Store covered in refrigerator.

*Tart can be served warm if desired.

High Altitude (3500–6500 ft): Bake 40 to 45 minutes.

1 Serving: Calories 240; Total Fat 16g (Saturated Fat 7g; Trans Fat 2g); Cholesterol 55mg; Sodium 280mg; Total Carbohydrate 19g (Dietary Fiber 0g) Exchanges: $\frac{1}{2}$ Starch, 1 Other Carbohydrate, $\frac{1}{2}$ High-Fat Meat, 2 Fat Carbohydrate Choices: 1

CREPES

1 box (19.5 oz) Pillsbury traditional fudge
   brownie mix
1 cup Pillsbury BEST® all-purpose flour
3 eggs, beaten
1¹/₂ cups milk
¹/₂ cup vegetable oil

FILLING

1 cup butter or margarine
¹/₂ cup granulated sugar
2 teaspoons vanilla
1 tablespoon finely grated lemon peel
6 large firm ripe bananas, cut into ¹/₄-inch
   slices

TOPPINGS

¹/₂ cup caramel topping
³/₄ cup frozen (thawed) whipped topping
2 tablespoons powdered sugar
¹/₄ cup chopped walnuts

Sherry Smith | Bunker Hill, WV

Sherry Smith's family loves pancakes and brownies, so she incorporated both in her new recipe. Her family deemed it worth entering. Sherry started cooking and baking when she was five. She also helped churn butter, make cottage cheese and preserve vegetables from the family garden. Sherry started a scholarship pageant program 16 years ago, which she still directs. She was active in the PTA at the state and national levels and was awarded an Honorary National PTA Life Membership.

banana-filled caramel-chocolate crepes

12 servings | Prep Time: **1 hour 25 minutes** | Start to Finish: **1 hour 25 minutes**

1 In large bowl, stir together brownie mix, flour, eggs, milk and oil until smooth.

2 Spray 10-inch skillet with cooking spray; heat over medium heat. Pour about ¹/₄ cup batter onto center of skillet. Immediately rotate skillet until thin layer of batter covers bottom. Cook over medium heat about 1 minute, turning once, until top appears slightly dry.

3 Remove crepe to cutting board, flipping crepe over so first cooked side is facing up. Immediately roll up crepe; place on plate to cool. Cover with kitchen towel. Repeat with remaining batter.

4 In large saucepan, cook butter and granulated sugar over medium heat, stirring frequently, until sugar is dissolved. Stir in vanilla and lemon peel until well mixed. Add banana slices; gently toss until coated and slightly softened.

5 Fill 1 crepe at a time, keeping remaining crepes covered. Gently unroll crepe; fill with slightly less than ¹/₄ cup banana filling. Reroll crepe; place seam side down on platter. Repeat with remaining crepes. Top crepes with drizzle of caramel topping and dollop of whipped topping. Sprinkle tops lightly with powdered sugar; sprinkle with walnuts. Serve immediately.

High Altitude (3500–6500 ft): Increase flour to 1¹/₄ cups. When cooking crepes, heat skillet over medium-low heat.

1 Serving (2 crepes each): Calories 610; Total Fat 31g (Saturated Fat 13g; Trans Fat 1g); Cholesterol 90mg; Sodium 190mg; Total Carbohydrate 75g (Dietary Fiber 2g) **Exchanges:** 2 Starch, 1 Fruit, 2 Other Carbohydrate, 6 Fat Carbohydrate Choices: 5

SYRUP

$^1/_4$ cup sugar

$^1/_2$ cup honey

$^1/_3$ cup water

2 teaspoons lemon juice

$^1/_8$ teaspoon ground cinnamon

Dash salt

3 whole cloves or dash ground cloves

NUT FILLING

$^1/_2$ cup blanched sliced almonds

$^1/_4$ cup chopped walnuts

1 tablespoon sugar

$^1/_2$ teaspoon ground cinnamon

Dash salt, if desired

BISCUITS

1 can (16.3 oz) Pillsbury Grands!® Flaky Layers Butter Tastin'® refrigerated biscuits (8 biscuits)

Wendy Connick I **Culver City, CA**

Wendy Connick says one of the best things about this weekend breakfast dish, aside from its great flavor, is that it can be prepared the night before and just popped in the oven the next morning. She remembers making French green beans with her mother when she was so little that she had a hard time seeing the stove top. Her worst cooking disaster: making pea soup in a pressure cooker and forgetting to release the valve before removing the lid. Wendy spent the rest of that afternoon wiping soup from the floor, walls and ceiling.

breakfast baklava

8 servings I Prep Time: **35 minutes** I Start to Finish: **1 hour**

1 Heat oven to 350°F. Generously spray 8 ($2^3/_4 \times 1^1/_4$-inch) nonstick muffin cups with cooking spray.

2 In 1-quart saucepan, mix syrup ingredients; heat to boiling. Remove from heat; cool 10 minutes. Discard whole cloves.

3 Meanwhile, in food processor bowl with metal blade, place filling ingredients. Cover; process with on-and-off pulses until finely chopped. Set aside.

4 Separate dough into 8 biscuits. Separate each biscuit into 3 layers. Place 1 biscuit layer in bottom of 1 muffin cup. Brush dough with syrup; top with $1^1/_2$ teaspoons nut filling and drizzle with $1^1/_2$ teaspoons syrup. Place second biscuit layer on top; press edge of second biscuit into side of bottom biscuit. Brush with syrup; top with $1^1/_2$ teaspoons nut filling and drizzle with $1^1/_2$ teaspoons syrup. Top with third biscuit layer. Brush with syrup; sprinkle with 1 teaspoon nut filling. Repeat with remaining biscuits. Reserve remaining syrup (about $^1/_2$ cup).*

5 Bake 18 to 22 minutes or until deep golden brown. Cool 1 minute. Remove from pan. Serve warm with remaining syrup.

*To make ahead, prepare as directed through step 4; cover and refrigerate overnight. Bake as directed. Reheat reserved $^1/_2$ cup syrup in microwave on High 30 to 60 seconds until hot.

High Altitude (3500-6500 ft): No change.

1 Serving: Calories 370; Total Fat 16g (Saturated Fat 3g; Trans Fat 3g); Cholesterol 0mg; Sodium 570mg; Total Carbohydrate 52g (Dietary Fiber 1g) Exchanges: 1 Starch, $2^1/_2$ Other Carbohydrate, $^1/_2$ High-Fat Meat, 2 Fat Carbohydrate Choices: $3^1/_2$

2 cans (8 oz each) Pillsbury refrigerated
garlic butter crescent dinner rolls (8 rolls
each)

1 package (8 oz) cream cheese, softened

3 eggs

1 small onion, chopped (¼ cup)

1 box (9 oz) frozen spinach, thawed,
squeezed to drain

¼ teaspoon salt

⅛ teaspoon pepper

1 cup shredded mozzarella cheese (4 oz)

breakfast quiches to go

16 quiches | Prep Time: **25 minutes** | Start to Finish: **45 minutes**

1 Heat oven to 350°F. Spray 16 (2¾ × 1¼-inch) muffin cups with cooking spray.

2 Separate each can of crescent dough into 8 triangles. Press 1 triangle on bottom and up side of each muffin cup.

3 In large bowl, beat cream cheese with electric mixer on medium speed until smooth. Add eggs, one at a time, beating well after each addition. Stir in onion, spinach, salt and pepper until well mixed. Fold in cheese. Fill each cup to the top with egg mixture (do not overfill).

4 Bake 15 to 20 minutes or until knife inserted in center comes out clean and edges of rolls are golden brown. Remove from pan. Serve warm.

High Altitude (3500–6500 ft): Bake 18 to 23 minutes.

1 **Quiche:** Calories 200; Total Fat 14g (Saturated Fat 6g; Trans Fat 2g); Cholesterol 55mg; Sodium 400mg; Total Carbohydrate 12g (Dietary Fiber 0g) **Exchanges:** 1 Starch, ½ Medium-Fat Meat, 2 Fat **Carbohydrate Choices:** 1

Diane Denny | Jacksonville, FL

"Anytime we need finger food for a party or picnic, our friends ask me to bring the quiche," says **Diane Denny** about her Bake-Off® recipe. They're portable enough to grab and go, she says, and kids love pressing the crescent rolls into the muffin tins. Raised in Louisiana, Diane was influenced by Cajun cooking. She earned her cooking stripes the usual way: by eating her mistakes. One mishap involved expired yeast. The result: extremely dense biscuits. "My husband teases me to this day about using them for skeet shooting," she says.

½ cup powdered sugar

1 package (8 oz) cream cheese, softened

1 tablespoon strong brewed coffee, cooled

½ teaspoon vanilla

1 can (16.3 oz) Pillsbury Grands! Flaky Layers refrigerated buttermilk biscuits (8 biscuits)

3 to 4 tablespoons butter or margarine, melted

¼ cup granulated sugar

1 jar (12.25 oz) caramel topping

¾ cup coarsely chopped butter toffee peanuts

2 teaspoons coffee-flavored liqueur or cooled strong brewed coffee

1 cup frozen (thawed) whipped topping, if desired

Linda Bibbo | Chagrin Falls, OH

Linda Bibbo's favorite ingredient is her homemade vanilla. She loves to bake, and with specialty coffee drinks and recipes being so popular right now, she says her entry will appeal to many. While she says she's had her share of baking disasters, this wasn't one of them. After serving the crunch cups at a family brunch, a friendly family feud ensued over the last remaining treat. It's always Christmas at the Bibbo house. Linda makes handcrafted ornaments and keeps a decorated Christmas tree on display in the dining room year-round.

caramel latte crunch cups

8 servings | Prep Time: **40 minutes** | Start to Finish: **1 hour 25 minutes**

1. Heat oven to 375°F. Generously spray 8 jumbo muffin cups or 8 (6-oz) custard cups with cooking spray.

2. In small bowl, beat powdered sugar, cream cheese, coffee and vanilla with electric mixer on medium speed about 1 minute or until smooth and creamy.

3. Separate dough into 8 biscuits. Press or roll each biscuit into 5-inch round. Brush one side of each round with melted butter. Sprinkle with granulated sugar; press sugar into dough. Press rounds, sugared sides down, evenly in bottom and up sides of muffin cups. Spread about 1 tablespoon cream cheese mixture evenly over dough in bottom of each cup. Drizzle each with 1 tablespoon caramel topping; reserve remaining caramel topping. Top with remaining cream cheese mixture; sprinkle with peanuts. (If using custard cups, place on large cookie sheet with sides.)

4. Bake 18 to 24 minutes or until edges of biscuit cups are deep golden brown. Cool 5 minutes. Remove from pan; cool 15 minutes.

5. Meanwhile, pour remaining caramel topping into small bowl; stir in liqueur. Drizzle over warm biscuit cups. Serve topped with whipped topping. Store covered in refrigerator.

High Altitude (3500-6500 ft): Bake 16 to 20 minutes.

1 **Serving:** Calories 630; Total Fat 29g (Saturated Fat 12g; Trans Fat 4g); Cholesterol 45mg; Sodium 790mg; Total Carbohydrate 81g (Dietary Fiber 1g) **Exchanges:** 2½ Starch, 3 Other Carbohydrate, 5½ Fat **Carbohydrate Choices:** 5½

2 tablespoons butter or margarine

1 box (9 oz) frozen spinach

1/2 teaspoon salt

1/4 teaspoon pepper

1 can (16.3 oz) Pillsbury Grands! Flaky Layers refrigerated original biscuits (8 biscuits)

4 oz thick-cut slices Canadian bacon, cut into 1/4-inch cubes

8 eggs

2 cups shredded mild Cheddar cheese (8 oz)

cheesy florentine biscuit cups

8 servings | Prep Time: **20 minutes** | Start to Finish: **50 minutes**

1   Heat oven to 350°F. Spray 8 jumbo muffin cups or 8 (6-oz) glass custard cups with cooking spray.

2   In 10-inch skillet, melt butter over medium heat. Stir in spinach, salt and pepper. Cook 5 to 7 minutes, stirring occasionally and breaking up spinach, if necessary, until spinach is hot. Remove from heat; set aside.

3   Separate dough into 8 biscuits. Place 1 biscuit in each muffin cup, pressing dough 3/4 of the way up sides of cups. Place heaping 1 tablespoon bacon on dough in bottom of each cup. Top each with spinach mixture. Using finger or end of wooden spoon handle, make 1 1/2-inch-wide indentation in center of each cup. Break 1 egg into each cup. Top each egg with 1/4 cup cheese (cups will be full). (If using custard cups, place on large cookie sheet with sides.)

4   Bake 20 to 25 minutes or until centers feel firm when touched and biscuits are golden brown. Cool 5 minutes. Remove from pan to serving plates. Serve warm.

High Altitude (3500–6500 ft): Bake 27 to 30 minutes.

1 Serving: Calories 420; Total Fat 26g (Saturated Fat 11g; Trans Fat 4g); Cholesterol 225mg; Sodium 1,130mg; Total Carbohydrate 26g (Dietary Fiber 0g) **Exchanges:** 1 1/2 Starch, 2 1/2 Medium-Fat Meat, 2 1/2 Fat **Carbohydrate Choices:** 2

Theresa D'Amato | York, PA

Theresa D'Amato created an eggs Benedict-style dish without hollandaise sauce. The hearty breakfast entrée is simple, and it may even help kids to "eat their spinach," she says. Theresa is a passionate bread baker. She loves making sourdough bread and focaccia, and once made 300 loaves of tea bread with friends in five hours to give as holiday gifts. She's proud of her home too—the second one she's built from the ground up with a builder. Her custom kitchen features a wood island that is so beautiful "I will never cut on it," she says.

STREUSEL TOPPING

2 tablespoons granulated sugar

2 tablespoons Pillsbury BEST all-purpose flour

1/2 teaspoon ground cinnamon

1 tablespoon butter or margarine

1/4 cup sliced almonds

DANISH

3 oz cream cheese (from 8-oz package), softened

1/4 cup powdered sugar

1/2 teaspoon vanilla

1 cup cherry pie filling with more fruit (from 21-oz can)

1/2 teaspoon almond extract

1 can (16.3 oz) Pillsbury Grands! Flaky Layers refrigerated original biscuits (8 biscuits)

3 tablespoons butter or margarine, melted

ICING

1 tablespoon cream cheese, softened

1/2 cup powdered sugar

1/4 teaspoon vanilla

1 to 2 teaspoons water

Jean Gottfried | Upper Sandusky, OH

The inspiration for **Jean Gottfried**'s recipe was beautiful pastries in the window of a local bakery. Her homemade version of the luscious, cherry- and cream cheese–filled Danish also has great eye appeal, she says—and they're easy to make at home. Jean is an active retiree, volunteering at a nearby elementary school, a hospital, a nature center and for the American Red Cross. She and her husband established a scholarship trust at the high school where she taught for 26 years, helping needy high school graduates continue their education.

cherry-almond streusel danish

8 Danish | Prep Time: **25 minutes** | Start to Finish: **55 minutes**

1. Heat oven to 350°F. In small bowl, mix granulated sugar, flour and cinnamon. Cut in 1 tablespoon butter, using fork, until mixture is crumbly. Add almonds; toss and set aside.

2. In another small bowl, mix 3 oz cream cheese, 1/4 cup powdered sugar and 1/2 teaspoon vanilla with electric mixer on medium speed until smooth. In third small bowl, mix pie filling and almond extract.

3. Separate biscuits; press each biscuit into 5-inch round. On center of each biscuit round, spoon pie filling with 4 or 5 cherries and heaping 2 teaspoons cream cheese mixture. Bring all sides of dough up over filling, stretching gently if necessary, and gather in center above filling; firmly pinch edges to seal. Dip tops and sides into melted butter, dip into streusel; lightly press streusel on tops and sides. Place seam sides down, 2 inches apart, on ungreased cookie sheet.

4. Bake 18 to 22 minutes or until golden brown. Remove from cookie sheet to cooling rack. Cool 5 minutes.

5. In small bowl, mix 1 tablespoon cream cheese, 1/2 cup powdered sugar and 1/4 teaspoon vanilla. Stir in water, 1 teaspoon at a time, until icing is smooth and creamy. Place icing in small resealable food-storage plastic bag; cut small tip off 1 bottom corner of bag. Squeeze icing in zigzag pattern on tops of cooled Danish.

High Altitude (3500-6500 ft): No change.

1 Danish: Calories 410; Total Fat 21g (Saturated Fat 9g; Trans Fat 4g); Cholesterol 30mg; Sodium 590mg; Total Carbohydrate 50g (Dietary Fiber 0g) Exchanges: 1 1/2 Starch, 2 Other Carbohydrate, 4 Fat Carbohydrate Choices: 3

1 Pillsbury refrigerated pie crust (from 15-oz box), softened as directed on box

2 tablespoons vegetable oil

½ teaspoon finely chopped garlic

1 medium onion, chopped (½ cup)

½ cup cooked real bacon pieces (from 2.5-oz package)

1 cup chopped cooked chicken

1 box (9 oz) frozen spinach, thawed, squeezed to drain and chopped

1 container (8 oz) sour cream

¼ teaspoon salt

¼ teaspoon garlic powder

⅛ teaspoon pepper

2 cups shredded sharp Cheddar cheese (8 oz)

1½ cups shredded Asiago cheese (6 oz)

3 eggs

½ cup whipping cream

Will Sperry | Bunker Hill, WV

Sautéing the onions is the hardest part of **Will Sperry**'s Bake-Off® recipe. Other than that, it's just chopping and combining, says Will. "It's easy to make and tastes great." A member of the Morgan Historical Committee, Will helps maintain the home of the first settler of West Virginia. Will did some cooking when he was young, including the time he burned down his parent's kitchen when making hash browns. He grew interested in cooking after he got married and gets most of his ideas from restaurant dishes.

chicken-asiago-spinach quiche

8 servings | Prep Time: **30 minutes** | Start to Finish: **1 hour 25 minutes**

1 Heat oven to 375°F. Unroll pie crust and press firmly against bottom and side of 9-inch regular or 9½-inch deep glass pie plate; flute edge as desired. Prick bottom of crust several times with fork. Bake 10 minutes; cool.

2 Meanwhile, in 10-inch skillet, heat oil over medium heat. Add garlic and onion; cook 2 to 3 minutes, stirring occasionally, until onion is tender. Reduce heat. Stir in bacon, chicken and spinach; toss to combine. Remove from heat; transfer mixture to large bowl.

3 Stir sour cream, salt, garlic powder and pepper into spinach mixture until well blended. Stir in cheeses.

4 In small bowl, beat eggs and whipping cream with fork or wire whisk until well blended. Gently fold into spinach mixture until well blended. Pour filling into pie crust.

5 Bake 15 minutes. Cover crust edge with strips of foil. Bake 20 to 25 minutes longer or until center is set and edge of crust is golden brown. Let stand 15 minutes before serving.

High Altitude (3500–6500 ft): No change.

1 Serving: Calories 550; Total Fat 42g (Saturated Fat 21g; Trans Fat 1g); Cholesterol 185mg; Sodium 760mg; Total Carbohydrate 18g (Dietary Fiber 2g) **Exchanges:** 1 Starch, 3 Medium-Fat Meat, 5½ Fat **Carbohydrate Choices:** 1

Pillsbury BEST all-purpose flour

1 can (10.1 oz) Pillsbury Big & Buttery refrigerated crescent dinner rolls (6 rolls)

1/3 cup creamy peanut butter

1/2 cup hazelnut spread with cocoa

2 firm ripe small bananas

1 egg white, beaten

1 tablespoon cinnamon-sugar (from 3.62-oz jar)*

Vicki Feldman | Manlius, NY

Looking back, **Vicki Feldman**'s fifth-grade teacher might have predicted that she'd be a Bake-Off® Contest finalist someday. Her assignment was to create a map of America, so she created a frosted sheet cake, cut in the shape of the United States. Vicki loves making cookies and cakes with interesting flavors and textures. She says this breakfast strudel looks quite elegant but is surprisingly simple to prepare and bakes quickly.

choco-peanut butter-banana breakfast strudel

16 slices | Prep Time: **25 minutes** | Start to Finish: **2 hours 20 minutes**

1 Heat oven to 350°F. Line cookie sheet with regular foil and lightly spray with cooking spray, or line cookie sheet with nonstick foil.

2 Sprinkle flour lightly on sheet of waxed paper. Unroll dough on floured paper into 1 long rectangle; press perforations to seal. Cover with another sheet of waxed paper; with rolling pin, roll to make 18×9-inch rectangle.

3 Spread peanut butter evenly over rectangle to within 1 inch of edges. Spread hazelnut spread evenly over peanut butter.

4 Cut bananas into about 1/8-inch slices; arrange slices with sides touching in 2 rows down center of hazelnut spread.

5 Fold in short ends of rectangle 1 inch. Starting at one long side of rectangle, roll up tightly; pinch edge of dough to seal. Remove from waxed paper; place seam side down on foil-lined cookie sheet. Brush with egg white; sprinkle with cinnamon-sugar.

6 Bake 20 to 25 minutes or until deep golden brown. Immediately transfer strudel on foil to cooling rack. Cool 30 minutes.

7 Loosely wrap foil around strudel; refrigerate 30 to 60 minutes or until chilled. To serve, cut into 1-inch slices, using serrated knife. Wrap and refrigerate any remaining strudel.

*One tablespoon sugar mixed with 1/4 teaspoon ground cinnamon can be substituted for the cinnamon-sugar.

High Altitude (3500–6500 ft): No change.

1 Slice: Calories 170; Total Fat 9g (Saturated Fat 2g; Trans Fat 1g); Cholesterol 0mg; Sodium 170mg; Total Carbohydrate 18g (Dietary Fiber 1g) **Exchanges:** 1 Other Carbohydrate, 1/2 High-Fat Meat, 1 Fat **Carbohydrate Choices:** 1

½ cup sweetened dried cranberries, coarsely chopped

1 cup orange juice

1 can (8 oz) Pillsbury refrigerated crescent dinner rolls (8 rolls)

32 cocktail-size smoked link sausages (from 16-oz package)

½ cup packed light brown sugar

⅔ cup chopped pecans

cranberry-pecan crescent sausage wraps

32 servings | Prep Time: **35 minutes** | Start to Finish: **50 minutes**

1 Heat oven to 400°F. In small bowl, mix cranberries and orange juice. Let stand 15 minutes.

2 Meanwhile, separate dough into rectangles; press each into 8×4-inch rectangle. Cut each rectangle into 8 (about 2-inch) squares.

3 Place 1 sausage on each square; wrap dough around sausage. Pinch edges to seal. Place sausage rolls seam side down in 13×9-inch (3-quart) glass baking dish. Bake 10 to 15 minutes or until light golden brown.

4 Meanwhile, drain orange juice from cranberries into 2-quart saucepan; reserve cranberries. Stir brown sugar into orange juice. Cook over medium heat 2 to 3 minutes, stirring occasionally, until sugar is dissolved.

5 Remove sausage rolls from oven. Pour orange juice mixture evenly over sausage rolls. Sprinkle with cranberries and pecans. Bake 10 to 13 minutes longer or until golden brown and bubbly. Serve warm.

High Altitude (3500-6500 ft): In step 3, bake 15 to 18 minutes.

1 **Serving:** Calories 120; Total Fat 8g (Saturated Fat 3g; Trans Fat 1g); Cholesterol 10mg; Sodium 210mg; Total Carbohydrate 9g (Dietary Fiber 0g) **Exchanges:** ½ Other Carbohydrate, ½ High-Fat Meat, 1 Fat **Carbohydrate Choices:** ½

Lisa Kramer | Madison, IN

Lisa Kramer adds humor when she cooks. Case in point: She started throwing ingredients together and came up with this recipe while doing an imitation of Julia Child. Her recipe is quick, easy, different and delicious. She tries to use ingredients on hand and add the unexpected. Lisa built the bookcases that hold 3,000-plus books in her home, and she constructed the table top in her kitchen to seat more people. As a teenager, she was playing big band music with professionals.

ROLLS

1/4 cup sweetened dried cranberries, coarsely chopped

1/3 cup chopped walnuts

1/2 cup granulated sugar

1 teaspoon ground cinnamon

1 can (12 oz) Pillsbury® Grands!® Jr. Golden Layers® refrigerated biscuits

1/2 cup mascarpone cheese or cream cheese, softened

1/4 cup butter or margarine, melted

GLAZE

1 tablespoon mascarpone cheese or cream cheese, softened

1 cup powdered sugar

1 to 2 tablespoons milk

Pamela Shank | Parkersburg, WV

Pamela Shank's recipe tastes like old-fashioned comfort food, but it's quick and easy to prepare. "It goes together in a matter of minutes and always turns out," says Pamela. Dried cranberries and walnuts give it an updated twist. Their big home is on 10 wooded acres; deer, turkeys, raccoons and fox frequent her yard. Stainless steel measuring cups are one of Pamela's favorite cooking tools and cinnamon is her favorite ingredient.

category winner

mascarpone-filled cranberry-walnut rolls

6 servings | Prep Time: **25 minutes** | Start to Finish: **1 hour**

1 Heat oven to 350°F. Lightly spray 8- or 9-inch round cake pan with cooking spray.

2 In small bowl, mix cranberries and walnuts; set aside. In another small bowl, mix granulated sugar and cinnamon; set aside.

3 Separate dough into 10 biscuits; press each biscuit into 3-inch round. Place heaping 1 teaspoon of the mascarpone cheese on center of each biscuit. Bring all sides of dough up over filling, stretching gently if necessary, and gather in center above filling to form a ball; firmly pinch edges to seal. Roll each biscuit in melted butter, then roll in sugar-cinnamon mixture. Place 1 biscuit in center of pan. Arrange remaining biscuits, seam sides down and sides touching, in circle around center biscuit. Pour remaining butter over biscuits; sprinkle with remaining sugar-cinnamon mixture.

4 Reserve 1/4 cup cranberry-walnut mixture; sprinkle remaining mixture over biscuits.

5 Bake 28 to 33 minutes or until biscuits are golden brown. Place heatproof serving plate upside down on pan; carefully turn plate and pan over. Let stand 1 minute, then carefully remove pan.

6 Sprinkle reserved cranberry-walnut mixture over coffee cake. In medium bowl, stir glaze ingredients until smooth. Drizzle glaze over top of rolls. Serve warm.

High Altitude (3500–6500 ft): No change.

1 Serving: Calories 530; Total Fat 26g (Saturated Fat 11g; Trans Fat 3g); Cholesterol 40mg; Sodium 610mg; Total Carbohydrate 68g (Dietary Fiber 0g) Exchanges: 1 1/2 Starch, 3 Other Carbohydrate, 5 Fat Carbohydrate Choices: 4 1/2

ROLLS

1 egg

¼ cup orange crème fat-free yogurt (from 6-oz container)

1 can (13.9 oz) Pillsbury refrigerated orange flavor sweet rolls with icing (8 rolls)

SAUCE

Icing from can of sweet rolls

2 tablespoons butter or margarine

1 tablespoon orange juice

½ teaspoon almond extract

¼ cup orange marmalade

¼ cup sliced almonds

Melinda Moore | Albuquerque, NM

"My family never wholly agrees that a meal is good," says **Melinda Moore**. "There is always one voice of dissent." So when she served this recipe for a special weekend breakfast, Melinda was surprised and thrilled when everybody liked it. Her father was touched to learn he had inspired her recipe. Melinda explains that, when she was a girl, her dad always had fixed crêpes suzette on Sundays. When he substituted almond extract for the vanilla, the almond-orange sauce became a favorite.

orange-almond breakfast bake

8 servings | Prep Time: **20 minutes** | Start to Finish: **35 minutes**

1 Heat oven to 400°F. Spray bottom only of 13×9-inch (3-quart) glass baking dish with cooking spray.

2 In small bowl, beat egg with fork or wire whisk; stir in yogurt until smooth.

3 Unroll dough on cutting board. Set icing aside. Cut each strip in half crosswise. Dip each strip completely in egg mixture, then twist 2 or 3 times; place in baking dish. Bake 10 to 15 minutes or until golden brown.

4 Meanwhile, in 1-quart saucepan, heat icing, butter, orange juice, almond extract and marmalade to boiling over medium heat. Reduce heat to medium-low; cook 2 to 3 minutes, stirring occasionally, until slightly thickened and shiny. Remove from heat; stir in almonds.

5 Loosen rolls from baking dish with spatula. Drizzle with sauce; serve immediately.

High Altitude (3500–6500 ft): Bake 15 to 20 minutes.

1 Serving: Calories 260; Total Fat 12g (Saturated Fat 4g; Trans Fat 2g); Cholesterol 30mg; Sodium 380mg; Total Carbohydrate 34g (Dietary Fiber 0g) **Exchanges:** 1 Starch, 1 Other Carbohydrate, 2½ Fat **Carbohydrate Choices:** 2

1/4 cup chopped pecans

1 can (8 oz) Pillsbury refrigerated crescent dinner rolls (8 rolls)

1/2 cup blueberry spreadable fruit*

1 container (6 oz) mountain blueberry fat-free yogurt

1 firm ripe banana, cut into 1/4-inch slices

1/2 cup whipped cream topping in aerosol can

1/4 teaspoon ground cinnamon

Fresh blueberries, if desired

Renee Heimerl | Oakfield, WI

Renee Heimerl always was amazed at the myriad ways cooks use Pillsbury refrigerated crescent dinner rolls. She challenged herself to come up with a unique use for the dough, and created this waffle recipe— just days before the contest deadline. Renee says it's a "great weekend morning treat . . . quick, easy and fruity!" She often mixes and matches recipes to make use of what she has on hand. Renee owned a successful portrait studio for many years. Since selling the business, she has more time to do fun things like cook.

quick and fruity crescent waffles

4 servings | Prep Time: **25 minutes** | Start to Finish: **25 minutes**

1 Heat oven to 200°F. Heat square or rectangular waffle maker. Spray with cooking spray.

2 Meanwhile, in 8-inch nonstick skillet, toast pecans over medium heat 5 to 7 minutes, stirring frequently, until lightly browned. Remove from skillet; set aside.

3 Separate crescent dough into 8 triangles. Place 2 or 3 triangles at a time on waffle maker, leaving at least 1/2 inch of space around each triangle. Close lid of waffle maker; cook 1 to 2 minutes or until golden brown. Place cooked waffles on cookie sheet in oven to keep warm.

4 In 1-quart saucepan, heat spreadable fruit and yogurt over medium heat 2 to 3 minutes, stirring occasionally, until hot.

5 To serve, stack 2 crescent waffles, slightly overlapping, on each of 4 serving plates. Spoon 1/4 of the fruit sauce over each serving; top each serving with 1/4 of the banana slices and 1 tablespoon of the pecans. Top with whipped cream; sprinkle lightly with cinnamon. Garnish with blueberries.

*Blueberry preserves can be substituted for the spreadable fruit.

High Altitude (3500–6500 ft): No change.

1 Serving: Calories 450; Total Fat 19g (Saturated Fat 6g; Trans Fat 3g); Cholesterol 10mg; Sodium 470mg; Total Carbohydrate 63g (Dietary Fiber 5g) **Exchanges:** 2 1/2 Starch, 1 1/2 Other Carbohydrate, 3 1/2 Fat **Carbohydrate Choices:** 4

1 Pillsbury refrigerated pie crust (from 15-oz box), softened as directed on box

1/2 cup finely crushed garlic and butter croutons

1 cup shredded Cheddar cheese (4 oz)

4 oz smoked turkey sausage, sliced

1 box (9 oz) frozen spinach, thawed, squeezed to drain and chopped

2 tablespoons finely chopped onion

1 cup crumbled feta cheese (4 oz)

4 eggs

1 1/2 cups half-and-half

1/4 teaspoon salt, if desired

1/8 teaspoon pepper

8 cherry tomatoes, cut into quarters

spinach, sausage and feta quiche

8 servings | Prep Time: **30 minutes** | Start to Finish: **1 hour 45 minutes**

1 Heat oven to 350°F. Place pie crust in 9-inch glass pie plate or quiche pan as directed on box for One-Crust Filled Pie.

2 Cover bottom of pie crust with crushed croutons; sprinkle with Cheddar cheese. Layer sausage slices on cheese; top with spinach, onion and feta cheese.

3 In large bowl, beat eggs, half-and-half, salt and pepper with wire whisk until well blended; slowly pour into pie crust.

4 Bake 45 minutes. Cover crust edge with strips of foil. Bake 5 to 15 minutes longer or until knife inserted in center comes out clean. Let stand 15 minutes before serving. Garnish with tomatoes.

High Altitude (3500–6500 ft): No change.

1 **Serving:** Calories 350; Total Fat 24g (Saturated Fat 12g; Trans Fat 0.5g); Cholesterol 145mg; Sodium 600mg; Total Carbohydrate 19g (Dietary Fiber 1g) **Exchanges:** 1/2 Starch, 1 Other Carbohydrate, 1 1/2 Medium-Fat Meat, 3 Fat Carbohydrate Choices: 1

Kathleen Haller | Baltimore, MD

Kathleen Haller often cooks and bakes for her church. She combined ideas from several different recipes to create this quiche for a St. Patrick-themed church breakfast, and received so many compliments that she knew she was onto something. It's an interesting entrée that offers a hearty start to the day and transports well, she says. Kathleen's heritage is Polish and Czech, yet she's been recognized by the Maryland State Arts Council as an educator in Hawaiian culture and dance. Kathleen collects cookbooks and Hawaiian artifacts.

SOUFFLÉS

1 can (10.2 oz) Pillsbury Grands!
  Homestyle refrigerated buttermilk
  biscuits (5 biscuits)

4 eggs

1/4 cup chunky-style salsa

1/2 cup sour cream

1/3 cup cooked real bacon bits (from 3-oz
  package)

1 cup shredded mild Cheddar cheese (4 oz)

GARNISHES

Chunky-style salsa, if desired

Sour cream, if desired

Norita Solt | Bettendorf, IA

Norita Solt enjoys baking, but cooking is her true passion. "Cooking allows me to experiment more and play around with food." She spends four to five hours in the kitchen every day that she's home. The focal point of the kitchen she designed herself is a 60-inch professional stove. Norita loves to cook "Iowan foods," such as pork tenderloin and corn, which she says is very versatile. She has created recipes for corn soup and corn dessert. In 2006, she cooked for weeks preparing 2,250 items for a fund-raiser.

sunny morning star biscuit soufflés

6 servings | Prep Time: **15 minutes** | Start to Finish: **55 minutes**

1 Heat oven to 350°F. Spray 6 (6-oz) custard cups or 6 (8-oz) ramekins with cooking spray.

2 Cut each biscuit into 6 wedges. Using 5 wedges for each cup, arrange wedges around side of each cup with pointed ends up to form a "star." Press dough lightly on bottoms and sides of cups (it is not necessary to completely cover bottoms and sides of cups). Set aside.

3 In medium bowl, beat eggs with fork or wire whisk until blended. Beat in 1/4 cup salsa, 1/2 cup sour cream and the bacon bits until blended.

4 Spoon 2 tablespoons egg mixture into center of each cup; top each with about 2 tablespoons cheese. Spoon remaining egg mixture over cheese in each cup. Place cups on large cookie sheet with sides.

5 Bake 25 to 30 minutes or until eggs are set and biscuits are golden brown. Cool 10 minutes. Garnish with salsa and sour cream.

High Altitude (3500–6500 ft): No change.

1 Serving: Calories 340; Total Fat 21g (Saturated Fat 10g; Trans Fat 3g); Cholesterol 160mg; Sodium 940mg; Total Carbohydrate 22g (Dietary Fiber 0g) Exchanges: 1 Starch, 1/2 Other Carbohydrate, 1 1/2 Medium-Fat Meat, 2 1/2 Fat Carbohydrate Choices: 1 1/2

ROLLS

1 to 3 teaspoons shortening

1 can (17.5 oz) Pillsbury Grands! Flaky Supreme refrigerated cinnamon rolls with icing (5 rolls)

$1/2$ cup pineapple topping, drained

$1/2$ cup dry-roasted macadamia nuts, chopped

TOPPING

Icing from can of cinnamon rolls

1 tablespoon coconut-flavored rum or $1/2$ teaspoon rum extract

$1/2$ cup toasted flaked coconut, if desired*

GARNISHES

Fresh pineapple rings or chunks

Fresh mint leaves

Patty Colon | Egg Harbor City, NJ

Since weekdays are always such a rush, **Patty Colon** likes to make a nice breakfast on the weekend. "As soon as you put cinnamon buns in the oven, everyone comes running," she says. These breakfast rolls are inspired by tropical flavors, including pineapple, coconut and macadamia nuts. Her children will inherit a great recipe box, she says, since she is German, Irish and Dutch and her husband is Puerto Rican. Patty's kitchen is decorated with her collection of old cranberry labels and scoops.

taste-of-the-islands breakfast rolls

5 rolls | Prep Time: **15 minutes** | Start to Finish: **40 minutes**

1 Heat oven to 350°F. Grease cookie sheet with shortening.

2 Unroll cinnamon roll dough, cinnamon side up. Set icing aside. Spoon pineapple topping evenly over cinnamon rolls. Sprinkle nuts over pineapple topping.

3 Reroll dough into pinwheel shape; separate into 5 rolls. Place 2 inches apart on cookie sheet.

4 Bake 20 to 23 minutes or until golden brown.

5 Pour icing into small bowl; stir in rum. Spread icing on rolls; sprinkle with coconut. Place on serving platter; garnish with pineapple rings and mint.

*To toast coconut, heat oven to 350°F. Spread coconut in ungreased shallow pan. Bake uncovered 5 to 7 minutes, stirring occasionally, until golden brown.

High Altitude (3500–6500 ft): Heat oven to 325°F. Decrease pineapple topping to $1/4$ cup. Bake 22 to 25 minutes.

1 Roll: Calories 560; Total Fat 28g (Saturated Fat 7g; Trans Fat 5g); Cholesterol 0mg; Sodium 640mg; Total Carbohydrate 72g (Dietary Fiber 2g) Exchanges: 2 Starch, 3 Other Carbohydrate, 5 Fat **Carbohydrate Choices:** 5

FLATCAKES

1 tablespoon vegetable oil

1/2 cup chopped pecans

1 can (13.9 oz) Pillsbury refrigerated orange flavor sweet rolls with icing (8 rolls)

TOPPING

2 tablespoons butter or margarine

2 firm ripe medium bananas, sliced (2 cups)

2 tablespoons lime juice

1 cup fresh or canned, drained, pineapple tidbits

1 jar (12 oz) pineapple topping

1 can (15 oz) mandarin orange segments in light syrup, drained

ORANGE CREAM

1 1/4 cups whipping cream

Icing from can of sweet rolls

Audrey Madyun | Toledo, OH

Audrey Madyun's love for the flavors creamy orange and pineapple inspired her finalist entry. Her recipe is so simple that even a harried parent with little cooking experience could make it, yet it's elegant enough to serve at a ladies' brunch, Audrey says. She devotes any extra space at home, including two bedrooms, to her hobbies—baking, crafting and sewing. Audrey admits a fondness for pretty plates and dishes, too . . . and they've filled a closet. Herbs and veggies grow in her backyard.

tropical sunshine flatcakes with orange cream

8 servings | Prep Time: **30 minutes** | Start to Finish: **40 minutes**

1 Heat oven to 400°F. Generously brush 1 tablespoon oil on 1 large cookie sheet or 2 small cookie sheets.

2 Cut waxed paper or cooking parchment paper into 16 (6-inch square) sheets. Sprinkle about 1 1/2 teaspoons pecans on 1 sheet. Place 1 orange roll on pecans; sprinkle 1 1/2 teaspoons pecans on top of roll. Top with another waxed paper square. Using rolling pin, roll evenly until orange roll is 4 1/2 inches in diameter; remove waxed paper. Place roll on cookie sheet. Repeat with remaining rolls, placing 1 inch apart on cookie sheet. Set icing aside.

3 Bake 8 to 10 minutes or until golden brown.

4 Meanwhile, in 10-inch skillet, melt butter over medium-high heat. Add bananas, lime juice and pineapple; cook 1 minute, stirring frequently. Reduce heat to medium-low. Gently stir in pineapple topping; cook 3 to 4 minutes, stirring occasionally, until warmed. Gently stir in orange segments.

5 In medium bowl, beat whipping cream and icing with electric mixer on high speed until soft peaks form.

6 To serve, top flatcakes with warm pineapple topping and orange cream.

High Altitude (3500-6500 ft): No change.

1 **Serving:** Calories 560; Total Fat 28g (Saturated Fat 11g; Trans Fat 3g); Cholesterol 50mg; Sodium 380mg; Total Carbohydrate 72g (Dietary Fiber 2g) **Exchanges:** 1 Starch, 1 Fruit, 3 Other Carbohydrate, 5 1/2 Fat **Carbohydrate Choices:** 5

1/4 cup butter or margarine
1/2 cup caramel topping
1/4 cup packed dark brown sugar
6 cups sliced peeled Granny Smith apples (4 medium)
1/2 cup chopped pecans
1 can (16.3 oz) Pillsbury Grands! Flaky Layers Butter Tastin' refrigerated biscuits (8 biscuits)

upside-down caramel-apple biscuits

8 servings | Prep Time: **35 minutes** | Start to Finish: **1 hour 5 minutes**

1 Heat oven to 350°F. In 12-inch nonstick skillet, cook butter and caramel topping over medium-high heat, stirring occasionally, until melted and bubbly. Stir in brown sugar and apples. Cook over medium-high heat 12 to 15 minutes, stirring occasionally, until apples are tender.

2 Meanwhile, spray 8 (10-oz) custard cups or 8 (12-oz) ramekins with cooking spray. Sprinkle 1 tablespoon pecans in each cup. Spoon about 1/3 cup caramel-apple mixture evenly over pecans in each cup.

3 Separate biscuits; gently stretch each biscuit until large enough to cover caramel-apple mixture. Place biscuit on top of caramel-apple mixture in each cup. Place cups on large cookie sheet with sides.

4 Bake 18 to 23 minutes or until golden brown. Place cups on cooling rack; cool 5 minutes. Place heatproof serving plate upside down on each cup; carefully turn plate and cup over to remove biscuits. Serve warm.

High Altitude (3500–6500 ft): When cooking apples, stir frequently to avoid scorching.

1 Serving: Calories 420; Total Fat 20g (Saturated Fat 6g; Trans Fat 3g); Cholesterol 15mg; Sodium 670mg; Total Carbohydrate 56g (Dietary Fiber 2g) **Exchanges:** 1 1/2 Starch, 1/2 Fruit, 1 1/2 Other Carbohydrate, 4 Fat **Carbohydrate Choices:** 4

Laureen Pittman | Riverside, CA

Laureen Pittman enjoys improvising and creating new dishes to surprise her family and friends. Her mother-in-law is a fan of pineapple upside-down cake. Laureen tried apples and caramel instead of pineapple and served her recipe on her mother-in-law's birthday. "She loved it and said I should enter it." Laureen learned "just about everything about cooking" from her dad, a big, burly man who loved to cook. Her cooking specialty growing up was meatloaf. "My family loved mine better than Mom's, so I was assigned meatloaf duty every week."

Edgar Rudberg, St. Paul, Minnesota, was awarded $5,000 and a brand new range for his Salmon Pastries with Dill Pesto (p. 78). Pesto is Edgar's cooking specialty, and he likes salmon with dill.

chapter two

entertaining appetizers

These appetizer and snack ideas are perfect for serving at casual gatherings with family and friends or for holiday entertaining.

Trends in Entertaining Appetizers Category

Many appetizers featured dual textures and intense flavors.

Sweet and savory flavors were balanced with the use of jams and preserves. Jams and preserves—especially apricot, peach and blackberry—were used to prepare fillings and dipping sauces.

Spinach was the most popular vegetable. It was used in rollups, wraps, spreads, tarts, pockets and bundles.

Seafood was prevalent including crab, shrimp and salmon.

Figs, both fresh and dry, were a common ingredient.

The mini muffin tin was the preferred pan to create easy-to-hold, bite-size appetizers.

1 can (8 oz) Pillsbury refrigerated crescent dinner rolls (8 rolls)

1/4 cup apricot preserves

2 tablespoons butter or margarine

1/2 cup crumbled Gorgonzola cheese (2 oz)

1/2 cup chopped pecans

1/4 teaspoon freshly ground pepper

apricot-gorgonzola crescent appetizers

12 appetizers I Prep Time: **10 minutes** I Start to Finish: **40 minutes**

1 Heat oven to 350°F. Spray large cookie sheet with cooking spray. Unroll dough into 1 large rectangle; place on cookie sheet. Press dough into 13×9-inch rectangle; firmly press perforations to seal.

2 In small microwavable bowl, microwave preserves and butter uncovered on High about 30 seconds or until butter is melted; stir until smooth. Spread preserves mixture evenly over dough. Top evenly with cheese and pecans. Sprinkle evenly with pepper.

3 Bake 13 to 19 minutes or until crust is deep golden brown. Cool 10 minutes. Cut into 12 squares. Serve warm.

High Altitude (3500–6500 ft): No change.

1 **Appetizer:** Calories 160; Total Fat 11g (Saturated Fat 4g; Trans Fat 1g); Cholesterol 10mg; Sodium 230mg; Total Carbohydrate 13g (Dietary Fiber 0g) **Exchanges:** 1/2 Starch, 1/2 Other Carbohydrate, 2 Fat **Carbohydrate Choices:** 1

David Dahlman I Chatsworth, CA

By the time he was 11, **David Dahlman** often cooked family meals to help his mother. His grandmother was Czech, and a great cook. She taught David how to make traditional *kolachke* pastries with poppy seed filling for the holidays. He also remembers making lemon meringue pies using fresh lemons from the family tree. David now plucks his own tomatoes to make "fantastic homemade salsa," using balsamic vinegar in place of lime juice. He likes the classic pairing of fruit and cheese in this appetizer and says it's easy to make on short notice.

1¼ lb lean ground pork

1 can (8 oz) sliced or whole water chestnuts, drained, coarsely chopped

1 box (9 oz) frozen spinach, thawed, squeezed to drain

12 medium green onions, thinly sliced (¾ cup)

2 tablespoons soy sauce

1 teaspoon granulated garlic or garlic powder

¾ teaspoon ground ginger

¾ teaspoon white pepper or black pepper

2 eggs

2 cans (16.3 oz each) Pillsbury Grands! Flaky Layers refrigerated original biscuits (8 biscuits each)

1½ cups sweet-and-sour sauce or sweet-spicy chili sauce

Wendy Ko | Walnut Creek, CA

The Chinese pot stickers that **Wendy Ko** made as a girl inspired this recipe, which she made just once to test for this contest. Her entry puts an interesting twist on a Chinese dish that is friendly to all palates, Wendy says. Further, it's easy: simply mix everything together. Wendy's recently remodeled house was taped for an episode of a cable landscape show. Her most interesting trip involved visiting tuna facilities in Thailand—while she was pregnant. Wendy's favorite family meal is sushi.

asian pork dumplings

48 appetizers | Prep Time: **50 minutes** | Start to Finish: **1 hour 20 minutes**

1 Heat oven to 350°F. In large bowl, mix all ingredients except biscuits and sweet-and-sour sauce.

2 Remove 1 can of biscuits from refrigerator just before filling (keep remaining can of biscuits refrigerated). Separate each biscuit into 3 layers. Press each layer into 3½-inch round, being careful not to tear dough.

3 Spoon 1 rounded tablespoon of pork filling on center of each dough round. Bring all sides of dough up over filling, stretching gently if necessary, and gather in center above filling to form a dumpling; press gathered dough to seal. On ungreased large cookie sheet, place 24 dumplings 2 inches apart.*

4 Bake 17 to 27 minutes or until thermometer inserted in center reads 160°F** and sides and tops of dumplings are golden brown. Repeat to make remaining dumplings. Serve warm with sweet-and-sour sauce.

*To make ahead, cover and refrigerate unbaked dumplings on cookie sheet up to 2 hours before baking.

**Due to the natural nitrate content of certain ingredients such as onions, the pork filling may remain pink even though pork is cooked to 160°F.

High Altitude (3500–6500 ft): No change.

1 **Appetizer:** Calories 100; Total Fat 5g (Saturated Fat 2g; Trans Fat 1g); Cholesterol 15mg; Sodium 260mg; Total Carbohydrate 11g (Dietary Fiber 0g) **Exchanges:** ½ Starch, ½ High-Fat Meat **Carbohydrate Choices:** 1

1 package (3 oz) cream cheese, softened
1/2 cup crumbled Gorgonzola cheese (2 oz)*
1 can (8 oz) Pillsbury refrigerated crescent
  dinner rolls (8 rolls)
1/3 cup chopped pecans
1 teaspoon olive oil
1/3 cup finely chopped red onion
1 tablespoon balsamic vinegar
1/4 cup apricot preserves
1/8 to 1/4 teaspoon dried thyme leaves

blue cheese and red onion jam crescent thumbprints

32 appetizers | Prep Time: **30 minutes** | Start to Finish: **50 minutes**

1 Heat oven to 375°F. In small bowl, mix cream cheese and Gorgonzola cheese with fork until blended.

2 Unroll dough; separate into 2 rectangles, each about 11 inches long. Place 1 rectangle on cutting board; press perforations together to seal. Spread half of the cheese mixture over dough to within 1/2 inch of long sides; sprinkle half of the pecans evenly over cheese. Starting at 1 long side, roll up; press seam to seal. Cut roll into 16 (about 3/4-inch) slices with serrated knife; place cut sides down on ungreased large cookie sheet. Repeat with remaining dough, cheese and pecans.

3 Bake 14 to 17 minutes or until golden brown.

4 Meanwhile, in 8-inch nonstick skillet, heat oil over medium heat. Add onion; cook 3 to 5 minutes, stirring frequently, until soft and lightly brown. Remove from heat. Stir in vinegar, preserves (breaking up large pieces of fruit if necessary) and thyme; set aside.

5 After removing rolls from oven, immediately press back of a teaspoon into center of each roll to make small indentation. Spoon slightly less than 1/2 teaspoon onion jam into each indentation. Remove from cookie sheet. Serve warm.

*Gorgonzola is a creamy Italian blue cheese named after the town of its origin, but any type of blue cheese can be used in this recipe.

High Altitude (3500–6500 ft): Heat oven to 350°F.

1 Appetizer: Calories 60; Total Fat 4g (Saturated Fat 2g; Trans Fat 0g); Cholesterol 0mg; Sodium 90mg; Total Carbohydrate 5g (Dietary Fiber 0g) **Exchanges:** 1/2 Starch, 1/2 Fat **Carbohydrate Choices:** 1/2

Phyllis Weeks-Daniel |
San Diego, CA

Phyllis Weeks-Daniel loves salads with nuts, blue cheese and fruit in a balsamic dressing. She set out to make a recipe with those flavors, plus some crunch. When she served it, "All my tasters kept reaching for 'just one more.'" Phyllis uses her skills as a certified gemologist in custom designs for her clients. "Whether I use their gems or select new gemstones, to create an idea and then see a special piece of jewelry come to life is always rewarding," she says. Phyllis loves to bake and often plans dinner around dessert.

1 can (13.8 oz) Pillsbury refrigerated classic pizza crust

¹/₃ cup cream cheese (from 8-oz container or package)

¹/₄ cup crumbled blue cheese (1 oz)

1 cup shredded mozzarella cheese (4 oz)

4 slices prosciutto (about 2 oz), cut into thin strips

¹/₃ cup apricot preserves

blue cheesy prosciutto appetizer pizza

12 appetizers or 6 main-dish servings | Prep Time: **15 minutes** | Start to Finish: **30 minutes**

1 Heat oven to 400°F. Lightly spray large cookie sheet with cooking spray. Unroll pizza crust dough on cookie sheet; press dough into 15×12-inch rectangle. Bake 8 to 10 minutes or until light golden brown.

2 In small microwavable bowl, microwave cream cheese and blue cheese uncovered on High about 30 seconds or until melted. Stir until well mixed. Spread mixture evenly over partially baked crust. Sprinkle with mozzarella cheese; top with prosciutto.

3 In small microwavable bowl, microwave preserves uncovered on High about 30 seconds. Stir until smooth; drizzle over pizza.

4 Bake 8 to 12 minutes longer or until crust is golden brown and preserves in center of pizza start to bubble.

High Altitude (3500–6500 ft): No change.

1 Appetizer: Calories 170; Total Fat 6g (Saturated Fat 4g; Trans Fat 0g); Cholesterol 15mg; Sodium 410mg; Total Carbohydrate 22g (Dietary Fiber 0g) Exchanges: ¹/₂ Starch, 1 Other Carbohydrate, ¹/₂ High-Fat Meat, ¹/₂ Fat Carbohydrate Choices: 1¹/₂

Natalie Albert | **Wilton Manors, FL**

Natalie Albert has loved cooking since receiving an EASY-BAKE® Oven as a child. The excitement of creating something delicious for herself—a chocolate cake—made a lasting impression. Natalie first created this simple appetizer in the form of a pinwheel and served it at a friend's house. "Everyone said it was the best food there, but it looked messy," she says. By using a refrigerated pizza crust, Natalie managed to minimize prep time, improve on the presentation and achieve the same sophisticated combination of flavors.

2 cans (8 oz each) Pillsbury refrigerated crescent dinner rolls (8 rolls each)

6 slices fully cooked bacon (from 2.1-oz package)

1 package (6 oz) refrigerated cooked chicken breast strips, cubed

1 box (9 oz) frozen spinach, thawed, squeezed to drain and thoroughly chopped

1 can (13.75 oz) quartered artichoke hearts, drained, coarsely chopped

2 medium cloves garlic, finely chopped

1/2 cup mayonnaise or salad dressing

1/4 cup sour cream

1/2 cup shredded Asiago cheese (2 oz)

1/4 cup grated Parmesan cheese

cheesy chicken and artichoke bites

48 appetizers | Prep Time: **30 minutes** | Start to Finish: **50 minutes**

1 Heat oven to 375°F. Separate dough from both cans into 8 rectangles; press perforations to seal. Cut each rectangle into 6 (2-inch) squares. Press 1 square in bottom and up side of each of 48 ungreased mini muffin cups.

2 Heat bacon as directed on package; crumble. In large bowl, mix bacon and remaining ingredients. Place 1 tablespoon chicken filling in each cup.

3 Bake 12 to 20 minutes or until edges are golden brown. Immediately remove from pans to serving platter. Serve warm.

High Altitude (3500–6500 ft): Bake 16 to 24 minutes.

1 **Appetizer:** Calories 80; Total Fat 5g (Saturated Fat 2g; Trans Fat 1g); Cholesterol 10mg; Sodium 160mg; Total Carbohydrate 5g (Dietary Fiber 0g) **Exchanges:** 1/2 Starch, 1 Fat **Carbohydrate Choices:** 1/2

Noelle Kompa | Forest, VA

Noelle Kompa started with an artichoke dip recipe from her mother, then changed it with sour cream, chicken, spinach, bacon and Italian cheeses. Her resulting appetizer recipe is easy, tasty and versatile enough to serve at "casual or classy" occasions, she says. What's more, this is the first recipe she has created, says Noelle. An enthusiastic cook, she loves to try new recipes. Her specialties include appetizers and dinner. Her favorite kitchen tool? "I love my double oven," Noelle says.

4 oz cream cheese (from 8-oz package), softened

1/2 cup sour cream

1 teaspoon lemon-pepper seasoning

2 tablespoons chopped fresh chives

2 teaspoons small capers, drained

1/4 teaspoon salt

1 box (10 oz) frozen corn in a butter sauce, thawed

4 oz smoked salmon, flaked

2 cans (8 oz each) Pillsbury refrigerated crescent dinner rolls (8 rolls each)

creamy smoked salmon cups

48 appetizers | Prep Time: **30 minutes** | Start to Finish: **50 minutes**

1 Heat oven to 375°F. Spray 48 mini muffin cups with cooking spray.

2 In medium bowl, mix cream cheese and sour cream until well blended. Stir in lemon-pepper seasoning, chives, capers and salt. Stir in corn until well mixed. Fold in salmon.

3 Separate dough from both cans into 8 rectangles; press perforations to seal. Cut each rectangle into 6 (2-inch) squares. Press 1 square in bottom and up side of each mini muffin cup. Spoon slightly less than 1 tablespoon salmon filling into each cup.

4 Bake 10 to 18 minutes or until light golden brown. Cool 2 minutes; remove from pan to serving platter. Serve warm.

High Altitude (3500–6500 ft): Bake 16 to 20 minutes.

1 Appetizer: Calories 60; Total Fat 4g (Saturated Fat 2g; Trans Fat 1g); Cholesterol 0mg; Sodium 140mg; Total Carbohydrate 5g (Dietary Fiber 0g) Exchanges: 1/2 Starch, 1/2 Fat Carbohydrate Choices: 1/2

Sherry Klinedinst | South Bend, IN

"I believe that the culinary arts and the performing arts are related," says **Sherry Klinedinst**. "Taking an idea—whether it's a combination of musical notes and rhythms or a diverse list of ingredients—and bringing it to life is nothing short of just plain fun." Her recipe creation was inspired by a local restaurant that serves salmon dip with bread. Sherry keeps heavy-duty goggles in her gadget drawer for cutting potent onions. On the music side, she has composed and recorded three CDs.

1 Pillsbury refrigerated pie crust (from 15-oz box), softened as directed on box

6 dried figs or pitted dates, coarsely chopped ($^1/_3$ cup)

1 tablespoon packed dark brown sugar

$^1/_8$ to $^1/_4$ teaspoon ground cinnamon

$^1/_4$ cup chopped walnuts

$^1/_2$ cup crumbled Gorgonzola cheese (2 oz)

1 tablespoon honey

Lana McDonogh | **San Marcos, CA**

After seeing a previous Bake-Off® Contest winner on TV, **Lana McDonogh** informed her family and friends that she was going to enter "and win." "They all thought I was nuts. Not so funny now, huh?" Lana first made this recipe for Christmas. "I wanted to make a few new appetizers and came up with this recipe. Everyone loved them." Five years ago, Lana traveled to France and stayed in what was once Julia Child's home. She took classes from the new owner, a French-trained chef.

gorgonzola, fig and walnut tartlets

24 appetizers | Prep Time: **20 minutes** | Start to Finish: **35 minutes**

1 Heat oven to 425°F. Unroll pie crust on flat surface. Using 2-inch cookie cutter, cut 24 rounds from pie crust, rerolling crust scraps if necessary. Gently press I round in bottom and up side of each of 24 ungreased mini muffin cups.

2 In small bowl, mix figs, brown sugar, cinnamon and walnuts. Spoon slightly less than I teaspoon fig mixture into each cup. Break up any larger pieces of cheese. Top each tartlet with slightly less than I teaspoon cheese.

3 Bake 7 to II minutes or until bubbly and golden brown. Remove tartlets from pan to serving plate. Drizzle tartlets with honey. Serve warm.

High Altitude (3500–6500 ft): No change.

1 **Appetizer:** Calories 60; Total Fat 4g (Saturated Fat 1g; Trans Fat 0g); Cholesterol 0mg; Sodium 60mg; Total Carbohydrate 6g (Dietary Fiber 0g) **Exchanges:** $^1/_2$ Other Carbohydrate, $^1/_2$ Fat **Carbohydrate Choices:** $^1/_2$

1 box (9 oz) frozen spinach, thawed, squeezed to drain

1/3 cup garlic-and-herbs spreadable cheese

1/4 cup shredded mozzarella cheese (1 oz)

1/4 cup shredded 5-cheese or 6-cheese Italian cheese blend (1 oz)

3 tablespoons freshly grated Pecorino Romano or regular Romano cheese

2 tablespoons finely chopped shallot or onion

1/4 teaspoon garlic powder

1/8 teaspoon salt, if desired

1/8 teaspoon pepper, if desired

1 can (8 oz) Pillsbury refrigerated crescent dinner rolls (8 rolls)

24 paper-thin slices (about 4 inch diameter) smoked ham (from two 9-oz packages)*

Freshly grated or shredded Parmesan cheese, if desired

ham florentine mini-cups

24 appetizers I Prep Time: **30 minutes** I Start to Finish: **55 minutes**

1 Heat oven to 375°F. In medium bowl, mix all ingredients except rolls, ham and Parmesan cheese until well blended. Set aside.

2 Unroll dough. Separate dough into 4 rectangles; press perforations to seal. Cut each rectangle into 6 (2-inch) squares. Press 1 square in bottom and up side of each of 24 ungreased mini muffin cups.

3 Pat each ham slice dry with paper towel. Place 1 ham slice over dough in each cup (edges of ham will be higher than side of cup). Spoon rounded 1 teaspoon spinach mixture onto ham in center of each cup.

4 Bake 14 to 18 minutes or until crust is golden brown and filling is hot. To prevent excessive browning of ham, cover lightly with foil after first 5 minutes of baking. Cool in pan 1 minute. Gently remove from pan; let stand 3 minutes. Sprinkle lightly with Parmesan cheese before serving. Serve warm.

*For recipe success, whole paper-thin slices (about 4 inch diameter) of smoked ham (not shaved ham) are needed so slices can be easily formed into the dough-lined cups.

High Altitude (3500–6500 ft): No change.

1 **Appetizer:** Calories 80; Total Fat 5g (Saturated Fat 2g; Trans Fat 1g); Cholesterol 10mg; Sodium 260mg; Total Carbohydrate 4g (Dietary Fiber 0g) **Exchanges:** 1/2 Other Carbohydrate, 1/2 High-Fat Meat **Carbohydrate Choices:** 0

Patricia Ingalls I **West Paterson, NJ**

Patricia Ingalls loves making appetizers for family and friends. She's especially proud of this recipe and says the combination of cheeses and spinach complements the flavor of the smoked ham. "When they bake up, they almost look like small flowers." Patricia's heritage is Italian and Lithuanian—two very different cultures. She finds the food most interesting. Patricia learned to cook from her mom and three aunts "who visited often and cooked while staying with us. Watching each one gave me insights into a variety of cooking."

1 can (12 oz) Pillsbury Grands! Jr. Golden Layers® refrigerated biscuits

1 can (4.5 oz) chopped green chiles, drained

1/2 cup shredded Cheddar cheese (2 oz)

1/3 cup mayonnaise or salad dressing

2 tablespoons cooked real bacon pieces (from 3- to 4.3-oz jar or package)

1 teaspoon dried minced onion

20 pickled jalapeño slices (from 12-oz jar), drained

jalapeño popper cups

20 appetizers | Prep Time: **15 minutes** | Start to Finish: **40 minutes**

1 Heat oven to 375°F. Separate each biscuit into 2 rounds. Press 1 round in bottom and up side of each of 20 ungreased mini muffin cups.

2 In small bowl, mix remaining ingredients except jalapeño slices. Spoon heaping 1 teaspoon mixture into each cup; top each with 1 jalapeño slice.

3 Bake 13 to 19 minutes or until edges are golden brown. Remove from pan to serving platter; let stand 5 minutes. Serve warm.

High Altitude (3500–6500 ft): Bake 16 to 22 minutes.

1 **Appetizer:** Calories 100; Total Fat 6g (Saturated Fat 2g; Trans Fat 1g); Cholesterol 5mg; Sodium 290mg; Total Carbohydrate 8g (Dietary Fiber 0g) **Exchanges:** 1/2 Starch, 1 Fat **Carbohydrate Choices:** 1/2

Tracy Schuhmacher | **Penfield, NY**

"This is the kind of recipe I like to cook—it's quick, tasty and a little different," says **Tracy Schuhmacher**. Her entry incorporates the flavors of a popular appetizer but is much easier to prepare with no chopping and very little handling of the jalapeños, Tracy says. She cooks for her family almost every day. "Experimenting with recipes makes the task more interesting and fun," says Tracy. Her family's favorite meal is "family pizza night," when each member of the family makes his or her own pizza.

2 cans (8 oz each) Pillsbury refrigerated garlic butter crescent dinner rolls (8 rolls each)

1 cup finely shredded pepper Jack cheese (4 oz)

1/4 cup apricot preserves

1/4 cup chopped pecans

little apricot appetizer tarts

24 appetizers | Prep Time: **35 minutes** | Start to Finish: **1 hour**

1 Heat oven to 375°F. Spray 24 mini muffin cups with cooking spray.

2 Unroll each can of dough into a large rectangle; press perforations to seal. Cut each rectangle crosswise into 12 strips, about 1 inch wide. Place each strip in muffin cup, pressing dough to cover bottom and side, making sure all seams are sealed and forming 1/4-inch rim above cup.

3 Spoon 2 teaspoons cheese into each cup. Top each with 1/2 teaspoon preserves and 1/2 teaspoon pecans.

4 Bake 14 to 20 minutes or until crust is deep golden brown. Cool 5 minutes; remove from pan. Serve warm.

High Altitude (3500–6500 ft): No change.

1 **Appetizer:** Calories 70; Total Fat 5g (Saturated Fat 2g; Trans Fat 1g); Cholesterol 0mg; Sodium 120mg; Total Carbohydrate 6g (Dietary Fiber 0g) **Exchanges:** 1/2 Starch, 1 Fat **Carbohydrate Choices:** 1/2

Gail Singer | **Palm Desert, CA**

Savory tastes and simplicity make this recipe unique, says **Gail Singer**. It also uses Gail's favorite ingredient, pepper Jack cheese. She first served her recipe at a dinner party to accolades from her guests and husband. Now Gail makes it occasionally for dinner parties and when her husband requests it. Gail's first memories of cooking are with her grandmother. "We pulled strudel over the entire tablecloth and then rolled it with sugar and walnuts," she recalls.

1 tablespoon olive oil

1 medium onion, chopped (½ cup)

1 firm ripe mango, seed removed, peeled and cut into ¼-inch pieces (1 cup)

⅓ cup orange marmalade

1 tablespoon Dijon mustard

2 tablespoons balsamic vinegar

1 to 2 teaspoons soy sauce

1 can (13.8 oz) Pillsbury refrigerated classic pizza crust

4 oz thinly sliced prosciutto

1 cup shredded mozzarella cheese (4 oz)

1 cup crumbled goat (chèvre) cheese (4 oz)

Julie Pando | Watertown, MA

A pressed sandwich with fig spread, prosciutto and fresh mozzarella inspired **Julie Pando**'s appetizer recipe. Julie loves to read lots of recipes for a particular dish, then take the best elements of each and create her own. Of Albanian heritage, Julie prepares the interesting Albanian dishes that her mom and grandmother taught her, including drop (roll the "r" as you say it, she says), a sweet stuffing made from bread, butter, sugar and raisins. "It isn't Thanksgiving in our house without a bowl of drop on the table," says Julie.

mango, prosciutto and goat cheese appetizer pizza

24 appetizers or 6 main-dish servings | Prep Time: **20 minutes** | Start to Finish: **40 minutes**

1 Heat oven to 400°F. Heat 10-inch skillet over medium heat. Add oil and onion; cook about 5 minutes, stirring occasionally, until onion is softened and starting to brown. Reserve ½ cup mango. Stir remaining mango into onion. Cook 3 minutes, stirring frequently.

2 Stir in marmalade, mustard, vinegar and soy sauce. Cook 2 to 3 minutes, stirring frequently, until mixture thickens and most of liquid is absorbed. Remove from heat; cool while preparing crust.

3 Spray large cookie sheet with cooking spray. Unroll pizza crust dough on cookie sheet; press dough into 15×10-inch rectangle. Bake 8 to 10 minutes or until edges just begin to brown.

4 Spread mango-onion mixture evenly over crust. Top with prosciutto; sprinkle with mozzarella cheese and goat cheese.

5 Bake 8 to 10 minutes longer or until crust is golden brown and cheese is melted. Sprinkle with reserved ½ cup mango.

High Altitude (3500–6500 ft): No change.

1 Appetizer: Calories 110; Total Fat 4g (Saturated Fat 2g; Trans Fat 0g); Cholesterol 10mg; Sodium 260mg; Total Carbohydrate 13g (Dietary Fiber 0g) Exchanges: ½ Starch, ½ Other Carbohydrate, ½ High-Fat Meat **Carbohydrate Choices:** 1

1/4 cup peach preserves

2 teaspoons finely chopped red onion

1 teaspoon water

1/8 teaspoon ground cinnamon

1/8 teaspoon ground cloves

1/8 teaspoon ground nutmeg

1/8 teaspoon crushed red pepper flakes

1/8 teaspoon salt

1/8 teaspoon pepper

1 can (8 oz) Pillsbury refrigerated crescent dinner rolls (8 rolls)

1/4 cup cream cheese spread (from 8-oz container)

1/2 teaspoon balsamic vinegar

Laurie Benda | Madison, WI

With a busy life and young family, **Laurie Benda** couldn't locate the handset when she got her Bake-Off® call, so she made the best of things and continued via speaker phone. She likes this pinwheel recipe because it's a "flavorful bite" that uses simple ingredients and can be whipped up in minutes. "It's a complete twist on anything you'd expect from a jar of preserves," she says. A vegetarian, she often converts recipes from her favorite cookbooks into vegetarian versions.

peach chutney pinwheels

32 appetizers | Prep Time: **20 minutes** | Start to Finish: **55 minutes**

1 In 1-quart saucepan, stir together preserves, onion, water, cinnamon, cloves, nutmeg, pepper flakes, salt and pepper. Heat over medium-high heat until mixture begins to simmer. Reduce heat to medium-low; cook 1 minute, stirring frequently. Remove from heat; set aside.

2 Unroll crescent dough. Divide into 4 rectangles; press perforations to seal. Spread 1 tablespoon cream cheese over each rectangle, to within 1/2 inch of edge of 1 short end of rectangle.

3 Stir vinegar into cooled chutney. Spread 1/4 of chutney (about 1 tablespoon) over cream cheese on each rectangle. Starting at short end covered with cream cheese, gently roll up each rectangle. Pinch seam to seal. Place rolls on cutting board or large plate; cover with plastic wrap and refrigerate 20 minutes for easier slicing.

4 Heat oven to 375°F. Line 2 cookie sheets with foil; spray foil with cooking spray.

5 Using serrated knife, cut each roll into 8 slices. Place on cookie sheets. Bake 12 to 15 minutes or until golden brown. Immediately remove from cookie sheets. Serve warm.

High Altitude (3500-6500 ft): No change.

1 **Appetizer:** Calories 40; Total Fat 2g (Saturated Fat 1g; Trans Fat 0g); Cholesterol 0mg; Sodium 80mg; Total Carbohydrate 5g (Dietary Fiber 0g) **Exchanges:** 1/2 Other Carbohydrate, 1/2 Fat **Carbohydrate Choices:** 1/2

8 slices uncooked bacon

1 tablespoon olive oil

1 cup diced sweet yellow onion (such as Maui or Walla Walla)

1 large red bell pepper, diced (1½ cups)

¼ teaspoon salt

⅛ teaspoon pepper

¾ cup crumbled goat (chèvre) cheese (3 oz)

2 oz cream cheese (from 3-oz package), softened

1 tablespoon chopped fresh parsley

1 can (8 oz) Pillsbury refrigerated reduced-fat or regular crescent dinner rolls (8 rolls)

Alison Strunk | **Springfield, MO**

Taking inspiration from one of her favorite specialty pizzas from a restaurant, **Alison Strunk** created a recipe for gourmet-looking appetizers. Smoky bacon, smooth and tangy goat cheese, sweet red peppers and buttery, flaky crescent dough provide a great balance of flavors. The appetizer offers "great gourmet appeal," making it ideal for entertaining with style, she says. Plus, her recipe is easy and can be prepared in advance. Alison rarely makes this recipe, she says, "for fear that I would eat them all."

red pepper and goat cheese bites

32 appetizers I Prep Time: **40 minutes** I Start to Finish: **1 hour 5 minutes**

1 Heat oven to 350°F. Spray large cookie sheet with cooking spray, or line with cooking parchment paper.

2 In 10-inch skillet, cook bacon over medium heat 10 to 15 minutes, turning occasionally, until crisp. Remove from skillet; drain on paper towels. Crumble bacon; set aside.

3 Discard bacon drippings. Add oil to skillet; heat over medium heat until hot. Add onion and bell pepper; cook about 15 minutes, stirring occasionally, until soft and tender. Stir in salt and pepper. Place mixture in food processor bowl with metal blade. Cover; process until smooth. Or blend in blender on medium speed about 30 seconds, stopping once to scrape sides, until smooth.

4 In small bowl, mix goat cheese, cream cheese and parsley until smooth.

5 Unroll dough; separate into 4 rectangles. Press perforations to seal. Cut each rectangle into 8 (1½-inch) squares. Place squares on cookie sheet. Spoon rounded 1 teaspoon red pepper mixture on each square, spreading slightly. Spoon slightly less than 1 teaspoon cheese mixture on pepper mixture on each square. Top each with about ¼ teaspoon crumbled bacon.

6 Bake 15 to 22 minutes or until edges are golden brown. Serve warm, or refrigerate and serve chilled.

High Altitude (3500–6500 ft): Bake 15 to 18 minutes.

1 Appetizer: Calories 60; Total Fat 4g (Saturated Fat 2g; Trans Fat 0g); Cholesterol 5mg; Sodium 140mg; Total Carbohydrate 4g (Dietary Fiber 0g) **Exchanges:** ½ Starch, ½ Fat **Carbohydrate Choices:** 0

- ½ cup lightly packed chopped fresh dill weed
- ⅓ cup light olive oil
- ¼ cup chopped walnuts
- ¼ cup fresh lime juice
- 1 clove garlic
- 1 tablespoon Dijon mustard
- ⅔ cup shredded Parmesan cheese
- Salt and pepper, if desired
- ¾ lb salmon fillet, thawed if frozen and patted dry
- 1 box (15 oz) Pillsbury refrigerated pie crusts, softened as directed on box
- Dill weed sprigs

Edgar Rudberg | St. Paul, MN

This is the first recipe **Edgar Rudberg** has ever written down and he's glad he did. Edgar's finalist recipe is delicious, very simple and inexpensive—but gives "the feeling of gourmet," he says. It seems fancy, yet it's also economical, he adds. While in American Samoa, he learned how to roast a pig by heating large stones with a fire. He also camped for a month in the bush of Tanzania. Edgar is renovating his 1914 house.

category winner

salmon pastries with dill pesto

24 appetizers | Prep Time: **25 minutes** | Start to Finish: **50 minutes**

1 Heat oven to 400°F. In food processor bowl with metal blade or in blender, place chopped dill weed, oil, walnuts, lime juice, garlic, mustard, ½ cup of the cheese, the salt and pepper. Cover; process, stopping once to scrape side of bowl, until smooth.

2 If salmon has skin or bones, remove them; rinse fillet and pat dry with paper towel. Cut salmon into 24 (1-inch) cubes.

3 On cutting board, roll 1 pie crust into 12-inch round. Cut into 4 rows by 3 rows to make 12 (4×3-inch) rectangles. Repeat with remaining crust. (Rectangles cut at edge of crust will have rounded side.)

4 Spoon 1 level teaspoon dill pesto onto center of each rectangle; top with 1 salmon cube. Bring 4 corners of each rectangle over filling to center and pinch at top; pinch corners, leaving small openings on sides to vent steam. (For rectangles with rounded side, bring 3 points together at top, pinching to seal.) On ungreased large cookie sheet, place pastries 1 inch apart.

5 Bake 20 to 25 minutes or until golden brown.

6 Place remaining pesto in small resealable food-storage plastic bag. Cut small tip off 1 bottom corner of bag; squeeze bag to drizzle pesto over serving plate. Place pastries on serving plate. Sprinkle pastries with remaining cheese and garnish with dill weed sprigs. Serve warm.

High Altitude (3500–6500 ft): No change.

1 Appetizer: Calories 150; Total Fat 10g (Saturated Fat 3g; Trans Fat 0g); Cholesterol 15mg; Sodium 150mg; Total Carbohydrate 9g (Dietary Fiber 0g) **Exchanges:** ½ Starch, ½ Medium-Fat Meat, 1½ Fat **Carbohydrate Choices:** ½

TAQUITOS

3 tablespoons canola oil

⅓ cup finely chopped onion

½ bag (30-oz) frozen country-style shredded hash brown potatoes (4½ cups)

1 box (9 oz) frozen spinach

1 can (4.5 oz) chopped green chiles

1 teaspoon salt

1 teaspoon ground coriander

1 teaspoon garam masala

½ teaspoon ground ginger

1 tablespoon lemon juice

1 package (10.5 oz) flour tortillas for soft tacos and fajitas (12 tortillas)

SAUCE

1 jar (12 oz) apricot preserves

Remaining chopped green chiles

1 tablespoon cider vinegar

¼ to ½ teaspoon ground ginger

¾ teaspoon garam masala

⅛ teaspoon ground red pepper (cayenne)

Scott Hatfield | Grove City, PA

Scott Hatfield loves Indian food—especially samosas, his favorite appetizer. But since authentic ingredients can be hard to find in his small community, he came up with this samosa recipe that uses everyday ingredients. Best of all, it's a snap to make: Just chop an onion, thaw the spinach and roll the filing into the tortilla, he says. Scott enjoys the creative aspect of cooking. Although his kitchen is so small it sometimes feels like he's "cooking in a closet," he finds it relaxing and at times even meditative.

samosa taquitos with apricot chutney sauce

12 servings | Prep Time: **25 minutes** | Start to Finish: **40 minutes**

1 Heat oven to 400°F. In 12-inch nonstick skillet, heat 2 tablespoons of the oil over medium-high heat. Add onion and potatoes; cook about 10 minutes, stirring occasionally, until potatoes are thoroughly cooked and slightly browned.

2 Meanwhile, cook spinach in microwave as directed on box. Drain spinach; cool 5 minutes. Carefully squeeze with paper towels to drain. Pull spinach apart into smaller pieces. Measure 4 teaspoons of the chiles; reserve remaining chiles for sauce.

3 Stir spinach, 4 teaspoons chiles, the salt, coriander, 1 teaspoon garam masala and ½ teaspoon ginger into potato mixture. Cook over medium heat 2 to 3 minutes, stirring frequently, until mixed and thoroughly heated. Remove from heat; gently stir in lemon juice.

4 Place about ¼ cup potato filling on each tortilla, ½ inch from one side. Starting at side with filling, tightly roll up each tortilla around filling; place seam side down on ungreased cookie sheet. Brush taquitos with remaining 1 tablespoon oil.

5 Bake 8 to 11 minutes or until crispy and golden brown.

6 Meanwhile, in medium bowl, stir sauce ingredients until well mixed. Serve warm taquitos with sauce for dipping.

High Altitude (3500–6500 ft): No change.

1 Serving (1 taquito and 2 tablespoons sauce each): Calories 270; Total Fat 6g (Saturated Fat 1g; Trans Fat 1g); Cholesterol 0mg; Sodium 580mg; Total Carbohydrate 50g (Dietary Fiber 3g) **Exchanges:** 1 Starch, 2½ Other Carbohydrate, 1 Fat **Carbohydrate Choices:** 3

SAUCE

³/₄ cup mayonnaise or salad dressing

2 tablespoons mild chunky-style salsa

2¹/₄ teaspoons finely chopped chipotle chiles in adobo sauce (from 7-oz can)

¹/₄ teaspoon sugar

APPETIZERS

¹/₂ cup uncooked sushi (sticky) or medium-grain rice

²/₃ cup water

1 tablespoon seasoned rice vinegar

1 box (9 oz) frozen spinach

5 oz imitation crabmeat, shredded (1 cup)

¹/₂ teaspoon ground cumin

¹/₄ teaspoon sea salt or kosher salt

4 flour tortillas for burritos (from 11.5-oz package)

1 medium avocado, pitted, peeled and sliced

1 large or 2 small roasted red bell peppers (from 7-oz jar), cut into ¹/₂-inch strips

1 teaspoon lemon juice

3 tablespoons sesame seed, lightly toasted

Fresh cilantro sprigs

Jan Corby | Middletown, DE

Take your basic sushi, introduce it to zippy south-of-the-border flavors, wrap it inside a tortilla and you've got **Jan Corby**'s East-meets-Southwest appetizer. This recipe earned an enthusiastic thumbs-up from her husband, who proclaimed, "This is good stuff!" Jan once cooked for 40 soldiers in a primitive camp, as part of a historical reenactment. She prepared multiple courses, from roast turkey to mashed potatoes and pies, using only an open fire, a spit, a reflector oven and huge cast iron pots. "Great experience," she says.

---

south-of-the-border sushi appetizers

32 appetizers I Prep Time: **1 hour 5 minutes** I Start to Finish: **2 hours 5 minutes**

1 In small bowl, mix sauce ingredients until well blended; cover and refrigerate.

2 Rinse rice in cool water until water runs clear; drain well. Place rice and water in 1-quart saucepan. Heat to boiling; reduce heat to low. Cover; simmer 20 minutes (do not uncover). Remove from heat; let stand covered 10 minutes. Place rice in glass or plastic bowl; stir in vinegar. Set aside.

3 Cook spinach in microwave as directed on box. Drain spinach; cool 5 minutes. Carefully squeeze with paper towels to drain; set aside.

4 In small bowl, mix crabmeat, cumin and sea salt; set aside.

5 On each tortilla, spread 1 tablespoon of the sauce. Spread ¹/₃ cup rice mixture over half of each tortilla (if necessary, wet hands with cool water to prevent sticking). Top rice with ¹/₄ each of spinach and crabmeat mixture. Place avocado and pepper strips down center of each tortilla; sprinkle with lemon juice. Starting at filled side, carefully and tightly roll up tortillas. Wrap each tortilla roll-up in plastic wrap. Refrigerate at least 1 hour or up to 4 hours before serving.

6 To serve, trim ends from roll-ups; discard. Cut each roll into 8 even slices. If necessary, secure with toothpicks. Sprinkle cut sides with sesame seed. Place roll-ups on serving platter with small dish of remaining sauce; garnish with cilantro sprigs.

High Altitude (3500–6500 ft): No change.

1 **Appetizer:** Calories 90; Total Fat 6g (Saturated Fat 1g; Trans Fat 0g); Cholesterol 0mg; Sodium 140mg; Total Carbohydrate 7g (Dietary Fiber 0g) **Exchanges:** ¹/₂ Starch, 1 Fat **Carbohydrate Choices:** ¹/₂

1 teaspoon sesame oil

½ lb boneless skinless chicken breast, cut into ¼-inch pieces

4 medium green onions, sliced (¼ cup)

⅓ cup orange marmalade

1 teaspoon soy sauce

1 teaspoon cooking sherry, if desired

½ teaspoon garlic powder

½ teaspoon crushed red pepper flakes

1 can (8 oz) Pillsbury refrigerated crescent dinner rolls (8 rolls)

1 teaspoon sesame seed

spicy orange-chicken charmers

16 appetizers | Prep Time: **20 minutes** | Start to Finish: **45 minutes**

1 Heat oven to 375°F. Lightly spray 16 mini muffin cups with cooking spray. In 12-inch nonstick skillet, heat oil over medium heat. Add chicken and onions; cook 3 minutes, stirring frequently. Reduce heat to medium-low; stir in marmalade, soy sauce, sherry, garlic powder and red pepper flakes. Simmer uncovered about 5 minutes, stirring occasionally, until sauce is thickened and chicken is no longer pink in center. Remove from heat.

2 Meanwhile, unroll dough into 4 rectangles. Cut each rectangle into quarters by making another diagonal cut in addition to the perforation to make a total of 16 triangles.

3 Press largest part of each dough triangle in bottom and up side of muffin cup, leaving triangle points extending over cup. Fill each cup with about 1 tablespoon chicken mixture. For each cup, slightly stretch points of triangles to make longer; twist points together and place on top of filling. Spray shaped rolls lightly with cooking spray; sprinkle with sesame seed.

4 Bake 11 to 19 minutes or until golden brown. Carefully remove from pan to serving plate. Cool 5 minutes before serving. Serve warm.

High Altitude (3500–6500 ft): Bake 11 to 17 minutes.

1 Appetizer: Calories 100; Total Fat 4g (Saturated Fat 1g; Trans Fat 1g); Cholesterol 10mg; Sodium 140mg; Total Carbohydrate 11g (Dietary Fiber 0g) **Exchanges:** 1 Starch, ½ Fat **Carbohydrate Choices:** 1

Paula Naumann | Sleepy Eye, MN

Orange chicken from a Chinese restaurant is a favorite of **Paula Naumann**'s children. So is her appetizer recipe, which captures those "orange chicken" flavors. "They ate them up really fast and then told me to keep working on perfecting it," she says. But not because the recipe needed work: "They just wanted more." During her kitchen remodel in 2005, Paula cooked for her family of seven using only an electric skillet and a microwave in her family room . . . for 10 weeks.

3 tablespoons cream cheese spread (from 8-oz container)

1 teaspoon soy sauce

1/4 teaspoon ground ginger

1/2 teaspoon finely chopped garlic

1 can (8 oz) Pillsbury refrigerated butter flake crescent dinner rolls (8 rolls)

16 uncooked deveined peeled large shrimp (about 1/2 lb), thawed if frozen, tails removed, if desired

3 tablespoons sesame seed

1/3 cup apricot preserves

Margaret Blount | Morehead City, NC

For **Margaret Blount**, one of the benefits of living in a North Carolina coastal town is having ready access to fresh, high-quality shrimp—the starring ingredient of these simple but elegant appetizers. She says the shrimp makes this appetizer "company special, without a lot of trouble." When Margaret cooks, she tries to make the foods that have eye appeal, good aroma and memorable taste. Her son-in-law served as taste-tester when she was developing these bite-size treats. He found them "just too good to leave alone."

sweet-and-sour shrimp puffs

16 appetizers | Prep Time: **20 minutes** | Start to Finish: **45 minutes**

1 Heat oven to 375°F. Spray cookie sheet with cooking spray, or line with cooking parchment paper. In small bowl, mix cream cheese, soy sauce, ginger and garlic until well blended; set aside.

2 Separate dough into 8 triangles. Cut each triangle lengthwise in half to make 16 triangles. Spread about 1/2 teaspoon cream cheese mixture on each triangle. Pat shrimp dry with paper towels. Place 1 shrimp on shortest side of each triangle; roll up, starting at shortest side, rolling to opposite point.

3 Place sesame seed in small bowl. Gently press top of each roll into sesame seed; place roll, point side down, on cookie sheet.

4 Bake 16 to 21 minutes or until golden brown.

5 In small microwavable bowl, microwave preserves uncovered on High about 20 seconds or until melted. Gently spread 1 teaspoon melted preserves over each puff to glaze. Cool 5 minutes. Serve warm.

High Altitude (3500–6500 ft): No change.

1 **Appetizer:** Calories 100; Total Fat 5g (Saturated Fat 2g; Trans Fat 1g); Cholesterol 25mg; Sodium 170mg; Total Carbohydrate 10g (Dietary Fiber 0g) **Exchanges:** 1/2 Other Carbohydrate, 1/2 Very Lean Meat, 1 Fat **Carbohydrate Choices:** 1/2

1/2 cup chopped walnuts

1 can (13.8 oz) Pillsbury refrigerated classic pizza crust

2/3 cup basil pesto

1 box (9 oz) frozen spinach, thawed, squeezed to drain

1/2 cup sun-dried tomatoes in oil, patted dry, cut into 1/4-inch slices

1/2 cup well-drained artichoke hearts (from 14-oz can), coarsely chopped

1 cup crumbled feta cheese (4 oz)

1 cup shredded mozzarella cheese (4 oz)

Jennifer Harkleroad |
Jacksonville, FL

Since **Jennifer Harkleroad** visited Italy in 2006, she's been experimenting with new takes on pizza. She also loves pesto and works it into every recipe she can. She first served this simple recipe to girlfriends when hosting their weekly "Grey's Anatomy" get-together. "Everyone loved it!" she says. Jennifer has fond memories of making Christmas cookies, especially kiffles, with her mother.

toasted tuscan walnut squares

24 appetizers | Prep Time: **25 minutes** | Start to Finish: **55 minutes**

1 Heat oven to 400°F. Spread walnuts in ungreased shallow pan. Bake 3 to 7 minutes, stirring occasionally, until light brown. Set aside.

2 Lightly spray large cookie sheet or 15×10-inch pan with cooking spray. Unroll pizza crust dough on cookie sheet; press dough to 15×10-inch rectangle. Bake 8 to 12 minutes or until edges are light golden brown.

3 Spread pesto evenly over partially baked crust. Top evenly with spinach, tomatoes, artichoke hearts, feta cheese and mozzarella cheese.

4 Bake 8 to 15 minutes longer or until crust is golden brown and cheese is melted. Sprinkle with walnuts. Cut into 24 squares. Serve warm.

High Altitude (3500–6500 ft): No change.

1 Appetizer: Calories 130; Total Fat 8g (Saturated Fat 3g; Trans Fat 0g); Cholesterol 10mg; Sodium 270mg; Total Carbohydrate 10g (Dietary Fiber 0g) **Exchanges:** 1/2 Starch, 1/2 Medium-Fat Meat, 1 Fat **Carbohydrate Choices:** 1/2

1 can (13.8 oz) Pillsbury refrigerated classic pizza crust
1 package (8 oz) cream cheese, softened
1/4 cup mayonnaise or salad dressing
1/2 teaspoon Chinese hot mustard, if desired
1/4 teaspoon garlic salt
1 can (8 oz) sliced water chestnuts, drained, coarsely chopped
1 can (6 oz) lump crabmeat, drained
1/4 cup pineapple topping
2 cups shredded Monterey Jack cheese (8 oz)
4 medium green onions, chopped (1/4 cup)

Jasmine Buliga | Braintree, MA

Inspiration for this recipe, says **Jasmine Buliga**, came from one of her favorite Chinese appetizers. A pizza crust replaces won ton wrappers, and pineapple sauce stands in for duck plum sauce. One of the family's favorite meals is "build your own sandwich" night, which allows everyone to customize their own creation while still sitting down together as a family. She describes herself as a messy though creative cook who is always interested in trying new and different things. Jasmine's son is a hockey goalie and she loves to watch him play.

tropical crab rangoon appetizers

12 servings | Prep Time: **20 minutes** | Start to Finish: **40 minutes**

1 Heat oven to 400°F. Spray large cookie sheet or 16-inch pizza pan with cooking spray. Unroll pizza crust dough on cookie sheet; press dough into 17×12-inch rectangle or press dough on pizza pan. Bake 7 to 9 minutes or just until crust is light golden brown.

2 Meanwhile, in large bowl, beat cream cheese, mayonnaise, mustard and garlic salt with electric mixer on medium speed until smooth. Stir in water chestnuts and crabmeat, being careful to break up crabmeat as little as possible.

3 Spread crabmeat mixture evenly over partially baked crust to within 1 inch of edges. Spoon small spoonfuls of pineapple topping over crabmeat mixture; spread evenly. Sprinkle with Monterey Jack cheese and onions.

4 Bake 12 to 15 minutes longer or until cheese is bubbly and crust is golden brown. Cool 5 to 10 minutes before cutting.

High Altitude (3500–6500 ft): No change.

1 Serving: Calories 290; Total Fat 17g (Saturated Fat 9g; Trans Fat 0g); Cholesterol 50mg; Sodium 480mg; Total Carbohydrate 23g (Dietary Fiber 0g) **Exchanges:** 1 Starch, 1/2 Other Carbohydrate, 1 High-Fat Meat, 1 1/2 Fat **Carbohydrate Choices:** 1 1/2

- 1 Pillsbury refrigerated pie crust (from 15-oz box), softened as directed on box
- 2 packages (3 oz each) cream cheese, softened
- 5 teaspoons basil pesto
- 1 box (9 oz) frozen spinach, thawed, squeezed to drain
- 1/3 cup diced red onion
- 2 small tomatoes, thinly sliced
- 1 1/2 tablespoons dry-roasted sunflower nuts
- 1/3 cup shredded regular or smoked provolone cheese*
- 2 fresh basil leaves, thinly sliced

tuscan spinach and tomato "crustini"

12 appetizers | Prep Time: **20 minutes** | Start to Finish: **1 hour 15 minutes**

1 Heat oven to 375°F. Line large cookie sheet with cooking parchment paper, or spray with cooking spray. Unroll pie crust on cookie sheet.

2 In small bowl, stir together cream cheese and 4 teaspoons of the pesto. Spread cheese mixture evenly over pie crust to within 1 inch of edge. Arrange spinach evenly over cream cheese mixture. Sprinkle onion over spinach. Arrange tomato slices in single layer over onion. Carefully fold 1-inch edge of crust over filling, pleating crust every 2 inches. Brush remaining 1 teaspoon pesto over edge of crust.

3 Bake 20 minutes. Remove from oven; sprinkle sunflower nuts and provolone cheese evenly over filling. Bake 12 to 14 minutes longer or until cheese is melted and crust is light golden brown.

4 Cool 15 to 20 minutes. Sprinkle with sliced basil leaves. Cut into 12 wedges.

*Two slices (from 8-oz package) regular or smoke-flavored provolone cheese, cut into 1 1/4 × 1/8-inch strips, can be substituted for the shredded provolone cheese.

High Altitude (3500–6500 ft): In step 3, increase second bake time to 14 to 16 minutes.

1 **Appetizer:** Calories 170; Total Fat 12g (Saturated Fat 6g; Trans Fat 0g); Cholesterol 20mg; Sodium 180mg; Total Carbohydrate 11g (Dietary Fiber 0g) **Exchanges:** 1 Starch, 2 Fat **Carbohydrate Choices:** 1

Dianna Wara | Washington, IL

When friends called to say they'd arrive for a visit in an hour, **Dianna Wara** took stock. She had pie crust in the fridge, spinach in the freezer and tomatoes on the counter. Dianna threw together "crustini" with a Tuscan flair. "It's a crowd pleaser because it's uniquely different," she says. Dianna gets some of her best recipe ideas while driving. "I think of the ingredients I want to use, and plan out what I want the dish to look and taste like." Dianna also enjoys reading cookbooks from the 1920s to 1940s and contemporizing the recipes.

Vanda Pozzanghera, Pittsford, New York, won $5,000 and a brand new range for her Mexican Pesto-Pork Tacos (p. 112). Judges liked how the pesto gave these tacos a new flavor dimension.

chapter three

Old El Paso® Mexican favorites

For a casual snack or meal, try a taco, burrito, enchilada, tostado or other dish inspired by south-of-the-border flavors.

Trends in Mexican Favorites Category

Mole sauce was very popular, often made by combining enchilada sauce with chocolate syrup or cocoa, or for a mole with a twist, peanut butter.

Mexican cuisine was combined with Asian, Mediterranean, Indian and other foods from around the world to create unique dishes, such as sushi tacos, Mexican egg rolls and curry burritos.

Crushed taco shells replaced bread crumbs as coatings for chicken and fish and toppings for casseroles.

Chipotle peppers were the most widely used. Several recipes called for ancho, pasilla and poblano peppers while some listed serrano and piquillo peppers.

There was increased use of Mexican cheeses and dairy products, including queso fresco, Crema Mexicana, cotija and quesadilla.

SALSA

2 cups chopped plum (Roma) tomatoes (6 medium)

1 jalapeño chile, seeded, finely diced (2 tablespoons)

³/₄ cup pineapple topping

Salt and pepper to taste, if desired

TACOS

2 boxes (4.7 oz each) taco shells that stand on their own (10 shells each)

1 package (28 oz) frozen buffalo-style breaded chicken breast strips

¹/₂ cup mayonnaise or salad dressing

¹/₄ cup sour cream

¹/₄ cup pineapple topping

¹/₂ cup finely chopped celery

¹/₃ cup chopped green onions

³/₄ cup crumbled blue cheese (3 oz)

1 bag (6.5 oz) sweet butter lettuce or 1 head each red and green butter leaf lettuce

Annette Riva | Berwyn, IL

Annette Riva loves to cook and bake. "Nothing intimidates me—the more creative and interesting, the better," she says. Her finalist entry combines exciting sweet-spicy flavors along with soft and crunchy textures. It's simple, too, so you can have a great meal in no time, says Annette. If she had won the contest, Annette would have given a portion of the prize money to her church, taken her sons on a vacation to Italy, invested some and looked into opening a small café or dessert place. Annette says she is known for her baking and has baked many cakes for friends and family over the years.

buffalo chicken salad tacos with pineapple salsa

10 servings | Prep Time: **45 minutes** | Start to Finish: **45 minutes**

1 Heat oven to 325°F. In medium bowl, mix salsa ingredients (salsa will be juicy). Set aside.

2 Heat taco shells in oven as directed on box.

3 Meanwhile, microwave chicken as directed on package. In large bowl, mix mayonnaise, sour cream, ¹/₄ cup pineapple topping, the celery, onions and ¹/₄ cup of the cheese. Cut chicken into small bite-size pieces; add to mixture in bowl. Toss gently, coating chicken completely.

4 To assemble tacos, divide lettuce evenly among taco shells. Top lettuce in each shell with about 1 teaspoon salsa and ¹/₄ cup chicken filling. Top with remaining salsa and ¹/₂ cup blue cheese. Serve immediately.

High Altitude (3500–6500 ft): No change.

1 **Serving (2 tacos each):** Calories 550; Total Fat 29g (Saturated Fat 7g; Trans Fat 2g); Cholesterol 35mg; Sodium 1,130mg; Total Carbohydrate 56g (Dietary Fiber 5g) **Exchanges:** 2 Starch, 1¹/₂ Other Carbohydrate, 1¹/₂ Medium-Fat Meat, 4 Fat **Carbohydrate Choices:** 4

1 cup chunky-style salsa

1/4 cup creamy peanut butter

1/4 cup raisins

1 small chipotle chile in adobo sauce (from 7-oz can), seeded

1/2 cup chicken broth

1 clove garlic, finely chopped

2 tablespoons semisweet chocolate chips

2 tablespoons ground ancho chile pepper or chili powder

1/2 teaspoon pumpkin pie spice

1/4 teaspoon ground coriander

1 lb boneless skinless chicken breasts

4 flour tortillas for burritos (from 11.5-oz package)

1 avocado, pitted, peeled and thinly sliced

1/2 cup crumbled queso fresco cheese or fresh mozzarella cheese

1/2 cup sour cream

chicken mole poblano

4 servings | Prep Time: **20 minutes** | Start to Finish: **45 minutes**

1 In blender or food processor, place salsa, peanut butter, raisins, chipotle chile, broth, garlic, chocolate chips, ground chile pepper, pumpkin pie spice and coriander. Cover; blend until smooth.

2 In 12-inch skillet, place chicken breasts; add salsa mixture. Heat to boiling over medium heat, turning chicken occasionally to coat with sauce. Reduce heat to low. Cover; simmer about 20 minutes, stirring sauce occasionally, until juice of chicken is clear when center of thickest part is cut (170°F). Remove chicken from skillet to cutting board; cut crosswise into 1/4-inch slices. Return chicken to skillet; stir to coat with sauce.

3 Heat tortillas as directed on package. To serve, place each tortilla on serving plate; spoon 1/4 of the chicken and sauce mixture onto each tortilla. Top with avocado, cheese and sour cream. Fold tortillas in half over filling. Serve immediately.

High Altitude (3500–6500 ft): No change.

1 Serving: Calories 630; Total Fat 32g (Saturated Fat 10g; Trans Fat 2g); Cholesterol 95mg; Sodium 1,140mg; Total Carbohydrate 48g (Dietary Fiber 6g) **Exchanges:** 2 Starch, 1 Other Carbohydrate, 4 1/2 Very Lean Meat, 5 1/2 Fat **Carbohydrate Choices:** 3

DeAnn Hilterbrand |
Salt Lake City, UT

DeAnn Hilterbrand thinks mole is a Mexican culinary treasure that deserves more attention in American kitchens. It's one of the featured flavors in her simple, savory Mexican chicken recipe that "tastes like a special party dish that took hours to prepare." With four kids, DeAnn doesn't have a lot of time to fuss, but her fascination with all things food-related has caught on with her kids. "My three-year-old brings me dessert cookbooks with delicious-looking photographs to read for his bedtime story!" she says.

2 teaspoons grated lime peel

¼ cup fresh lime juice

2 cloves garlic, finely chopped

1 tablespoon finely chopped fresh cilantro

½ teaspoon crushed red pepper flakes

5 tablespoons olive oil

1 lb boneless pork loin chops (½ inch thick)
   or pork tenderloin, cut into ½-inch cubes

2 small onions, thinly sliced

1 can (16 oz) fat-free refried beans

1 package (11.5 oz) flour tortillas for burritos
   (8 tortillas)

2 cups finely shredded pepper Jack or
   Monterey Jack cheese (8 oz)

1 to 1½ cups chunky-style salsa

1 container (8 oz) sour cream

Kimberly Fluck | Canon City, CO

Kimberly Fluck developed a passion for cooking by watching television cooking shows. While she usually starts with an existing recipe and tweaks it, these pork roll-ups were entirely her own creation. The combined flavors of fresh cilantro and lime juice, along with mellow and sweet caramelized onions, make it fresh tasting and flavorful, she says. When Kimberly's in the kitchen, beautiful handcrafted stained glass windows and panels surround her.

cilantro-lime pork roll-ups with caramelized onions

8 servings | Prep Time: **50 minutes** | Start to Finish: **1 hour 15 minutes**

1   In large resealable food-storage plastic bag, mix lime peel, lime juice, garlic, cilantro, red pepper flakes and 1 tablespoon of the oil. Add pork; seal bag and turn to coat with lime mixture. Refrigerate 30 minutes to 2 hours to marinate.

2   In 12-inch nonstick skillet, heat 1 tablespoon of the oil over medium heat. Add onions; cook 7 to 10 minutes, stirring frequently, until onions turn golden brown. Remove onions from skillet; keep warm.

3   Heat oven to 375°F. Remove pork from marinade; drain pork on paper towels to remove excess moisture. Discard marinade.

4   In same skillet, heat 1 tablespoon of the oil over medium-high heat. Add pork; cook 5 to 7 minutes, stirring occasionally, until no longer pink in center. Remove skillet from heat; set aside.

5   Brush 1 tablespoon oil on bottom and sides of 13×9-inch (3-quart) glass baking dish or 2 (8-inch square) glass baking dishes. In medium microwavable bowl, place refried beans. Cover with microwavable paper towel; microwave on High about 1 minute or until warm.

6   To assemble, spoon 2 tablespoons beans down center of each tortilla. Top with pork, onions and cheese. Roll up tortillas; place seam sides down in baking dish. Lightly brush remaining 1 tablespoon oil over tortillas.

7   Bake uncovered 18 to 24 minutes or until edges of tortillas are golden brown. Serve with salsa and sour cream.

High Altitude (3500–6500 ft): No change.

1 Serving: Calories 510; Total Fat 29g (Saturated Fat 12g; Trans Fat 2g); Cholesterol 80mg; Sodium 990mg; Total Carbohydrate 37g (Dietary Fiber 3g) **Exchanges:** 2 Starch, ½ Other Carbohydrate, 2½ Lean Meat, 4 Fat **Carbohydrate Choices:** 2½

ENCHILADAS

1 can (19 oz) mild enchilada sauce

1 cup whipping cream

2 tablespoons olive oil

1 small onion, coarsely chopped (^{1}/$_4$ cup)

1 box (10 oz) frozen corn and butter sauce, thawed

1 can (4.5 oz) chopped green chiles

^{1}/$_2$ cup lightly packed fresh cilantro, stems removed, coarsely chopped

^{1}/$_4$ cup dry sherry or apple juice

1 can (1 lb) pasteurized crabmeat or 3 cans (6 oz each) lump crabmeat, drained

10 flour tortillas for soft tacos and fajitas (from 10.5-oz package)

4 cups shredded Cheddar-Monterey Jack or Colby-Monterey Jack cheese blend (1 lb)

^{1}/$_2$ cup chopped green onions (8 medium)

1 package (2 oz) blanched slivered almonds

GARNISHES

^{2}/$_3$ cup sour cream

Lime wedges

Sharon Chittock | Grass Valley, CA

"Who doesn't like crab in a delicious Mexican-flavored cream sauce?" asks **Sharon Chittock**. She adapted this recipe from an often-requested family favorite. Sharon happily shares her gift for cooking, whether it's making her special 12-layer torte for a friend's birthday, or catering her niece's wedding, for which she says, "I cooked a meal for 130 guests with only one stove with one oven." She made oven-roasted potatoes and five huge pans of chicken, marveling that every-thing was done on time.

cravin' crab enchiladas

10 servings | Prep Time: **40 minutes** | Start to Finish: **1 hour 20 minutes**

1 Heat oven to 350°F. Spray 13×9-inch (3-quart) glass baking dish with cooking spray.

2 In 2-quart saucepan, heat enchilada sauce and whipping cream to boiling over medium heat, stirring occasionally. Reduce heat to low; simmer uncovered 7 to 10 minutes, stirring occasionally, until sauce is reduced and slightly thickened.

3 Meanwhile, in 12-inch skillet, heat oil over medium-high heat until hot. Add onion; cook 2 to 3 minutes, stirring occasionally, until softened and translucent (do not brown). Stir in corn, chiles, ^{1}/$_4$ cup of the cilantro, the sherry and crabmeat until well mixed. Remove from heat.

4 Spoon slightly less than ^{1}/$_2$ cup crabmeat mixture down center of each tortilla; top each with ^{1}/$_4$ cup of the cheese. Roll up tortillas; place seam sides down in baking dish. Sprinkle remaining 1 ^{1}/$_2$ cups cheese over enchiladas. Pour sauce mixture over enchiladas.

5 Bake 30 to 35 minutes or until bubbly around edges. Sprinkle with remaining ^{1}/$_4$ cup cilantro, the green onions and almonds. Serve with sour cream and lime wedges.

High Altitude (3500–6500 ft): No change.

1 Serving: Calories 530; Total Fat 35g (Saturated Fat 17g; Trans Fat 2g); Cholesterol 130mg; Sodium 990mg; Total Carbohydrate 26g (Dietary Fiber 2g) **Exchanges:** 1 Starch, ^{1}/$_2$ Other Carbohydrate, 3^1/$_2$ Medium-Fat Meat, 3^1/$_2$ Fat **Carbohydrate Choices:** 2

1 can (16 oz) traditional refried beans

1 can (14.5 oz) petite diced tomatoes, undrained

1 cup chicken broth

$\frac{1}{2}$ cup (from 14-oz can) unsweetened coconut milk (not cream of coconut)

1 can (4.5 oz) chopped green chiles

1 package (1 oz) taco seasoning mix

6 sticks (0.75 oz each) sharp Cheddar or chipotle Cheddar cheese

1 package (10.5 oz) flour tortillas for soft tacos and fajitas (12 tortillas)

2 tablespoons vegetable oil

$\frac{1}{4}$ cup chopped fresh cilantro, if desired

4 medium green onions, sliced ($\frac{1}{4}$ cup), if desired

creamy bean soup with taquito dippers

4 servings | Prep Time: **30 minutes** | Start to Finish: **30 minutes**

1 Heat oven to 450°F. Line cookie sheet with foil.

2 In 2-quart saucepan, stir refried beans, tomatoes, broth, coconut milk, green chiles and taco seasoning mix; heat to boiling. Reduce heat to low; simmer uncovered about 20 minutes.

3 Meanwhile, cut each cheese stick in half lengthwise to make 2 thin sticks. Place 1 cheese stick on one edge of each tortilla; roll tortilla tightly around cheese. Brush edges of tortillas with water to seal. Place taquitos, seam sides down, on cookie sheet. Brush each lightly with oil. Bake 5 to 7 minutes or until edges of tortillas are golden brown and cheese is melted.

4 Pour soup into serving bowls; garnish with cilantro or onions. Serve with taquitos for dipping.

High Altitude (3500–6500 ft): No change.

1 Serving (1$\frac{1}{3}$ cups soup and 3 taquitos each): Calories 650; Total Fat 31g (Saturated Fat 14g; Trans Fat 3g); Cholesterol 45mg; Sodium 2,450mg; Total Carbohydrate 69g (Dietary Fiber 9g) **Exchanges:** 4 Starch, $\frac{1}{2}$ Other Carbohydrate, 1$\frac{1}{2}$ Very Lean Meat, 5$\frac{1}{2}$ Fat **Carbohydrate Choices:** 4$\frac{1}{2}$

Sheila Suhan | Scottdale, PA

Sheila Suhan developed this recipe because she tries to create new bean dishes for her son, a vegetarian. She's made it many times since then, and her son takes it back to school with him. Sheila worked as a deli clerk and meat wrapper for many years. She then enrolled in college and earned a degree in nursing. Sheila's baking specialty is white cake with raspberry filling and whipped cream cheese frosting. Her stick blender is her favorite kitchen tool, and curry is her favorite ingredient.

1 package (11.5 oz) flour tortillas for burritos (8 tortillas)

¼ cup vegetable oil

1 medium avocado, pitted, peeled and diced

½ cup diced peeled jicama

½ cup diced firm ripe banana

1 large orange, peeled, sectioned and chopped

½ cup diced fresh pineapple

2 tablespoons diced red onion

1 cup coarsely chopped cooked deveined peeled shrimp

½ cup diced pepper Jack or Monterey Jack cheese

2 tablespoons chopped fresh mint leaves

3 tablespoons orange marmalade

3 tablespoons sour cream

2 tablespoons lime juice

1 tablespoon chopped chipotle chile in adobo sauce

¼ cup honey-roasted peanuts

2 cups shredded lettuce

2 teaspoons grated lime peel

Roxanne Chan | **Albany, CA**

Roxanne Chan likes to create attractive salads that have a blend of flavors and are fun to eat. She thinks this salad meets all those criteria, plus it's "kid friendly." This flavor fusion—including tart lime juice, tangy sour cream, sweet orange marmalade, savory adobo sauce, nutty peanuts, crunchy jicama and even a bit of mint—definitely covers a lot of taste territory. It's perfect for lunch and festive enough to kick off a fiesta, she says. Roxanne's most unusual cooking experience was cooking a 22-pound lobster.

---

fiesta fruit and shrimp salad stacks

4 servings | Prep Time: **55 minutes** | Start to Finish: **55 minutes**

1 Heat oven to 375°F. Generously brush each side of tortillas with oil. Place tortillas on cookie sheets. Bake 8 to 10 minutes, turning after about 4 minutes, until edges are golden brown and crisp. Set aside.

2 Meanwhile, in medium bowl, mix avocado, jicama, banana, orange, pineapple, onion, shrimp, cheese and mint.

3 In small bowl, beat marmalade, sour cream, lime juice and chile with wire whisk until well blended. Reserve 2 tablespoons marmalade dressing. Gently toss remaining dressing with fruit mixture until evenly coated.

4 Place 1 tortilla on each of 4 serving plates. Spoon heaping 1 cup fruit mixture onto each tortilla; top each with another tortilla. Brush reserved dressing over top of each tortilla stack; sprinkle with peanuts. Arrange shredded lettuce around each tortilla stack; garnish with lime peel.

High Altitude (3500–6500 ft): No change.

1 Serving: Calories 740; Total Fat 40g (Saturated Fat 10g; Trans Fat 2g); Cholesterol 95mg; Sodium 880mg; Total Carbohydrate 73g (Dietary Fiber 7g) Exchanges: 3½ Starch, ½ Fruit, 1 Other Carbohydrate, 1½ Lean Meat, 6½ Fat Carbohydrate Choices: 5

1 lb uncooked chorizo sausage links (casings removed) or bulk chorizo sausage

1 can (4.5 oz) chopped green chiles

1/2 cup chunky-style salsa

1 chipotle chile, chopped, plus 2 tablespoons adobo sauce (from 7-oz can chipotle chiles in adobo sauce)

1 can (13.8 oz) Pillsbury refrigerated classic pizza crust

3/4 cup crumbled cotija cheese or shredded mozzarella cheese

1 to 2 tablespoons butter or margarine

8 eggs

2 to 3 tablespoons chopped fresh cilantro

2 ripe medium avocados, pitted, peeled and sliced

Pamela Tapia | Smyrna, GA

Pamela Tapia likes making homemade pizza and loves Mexican food. "This is both together," she says. Her entry can be "breakfast, lunch, brunch or dinner," says Pamela. She describes herself as "an avid recorder of cooking shows." "I try to duplicate at least one recipe every weekend." Her favorite family meal is tortillas, rice, chile verde and tamales, which her grandmother made at Christmas. Pamela visited Madrid in 2000 and recalls a dinner where waiters sang opera and she was served a fish covered in crispy garlic slices.

huevos rancheros pizza

8 servings | Prep Time: **25 minutes** | Start to Finish: **45 minutes**

1 Heat oven to 425°F. In 12-inch nonstick skillet, cook chorizo over medium heat 8 to 10 minutes, stirring occasionally, until no longer pink. Remove chorizo with slotted spoon; drain on paper towels. Drain all but 1 tablespoon drippings from skillet. Place chorizo in medium bowl; add green chiles, salsa, chipotle chile and adobo sauce; stir until well mixed. Set aside.

2 Spray 13×9-inch pan with cooking spray. Unroll pizza crust dough in pan; press dough to edges of pan. Prick pizza crust thoroughly with fork. Brush reserved 1 tablespoon chorizo drippings evenly over crust. Bake 8 to 9 minutes or until edges are light golden brown.

3 Spread chorizo mixture evenly over partially baked crust. Sprinkle with cheese. Bake 8 to 10 minutes longer or until crust is deep golden brown.

4 Meanwhile, wipe out skillet. In skillet, melt 1 to 2 tablespoons butter over medium-high heat until hot. Break eggs and slip into skillet. Immediately reduce heat to low. Cover; cook 7 to 10 minutes or until whites and yolks are firm, not runny (eggs will cook together in skillet).

5 Cut pizza into 8 pieces. Separate eggs. Top each serving with 1 fried egg; sprinkle with cilantro. Serve with avocado slices.

High Altitude (3500–6500 ft): No change.

1 Serving: Calories 590; Total Fat 39g (Saturated Fat 14g; Trans Fat 0g); Cholesterol 245mg; Sodium 1,470mg; Total Carbohydrate 31g (Dietary Fiber 3g) Exchanges: 1 Starch, 1 Other Carbohydrate, 3 1/2 High-Fat Meat, 2 Fat Carbohydrate Choices: 2

VINAIGRETTE

1/2 cup cubed peeled mango*

2 tablespoons mango nectar (from 12.5-oz can)

2 tablespoons white wine vinegar

1 tablespoon fresh lime juice

1 tablespoon fresh orange juice

1 tablespoon honey

1/3 cup canola oil

BOWLS

4 flour tortillas for burritos (from 11.5-oz package)

1/2 teaspoon ground cumin

1/2 teaspoon salt

SALAD

4 cups cubed cooked chicken breast

1 1/3 cups cubed peeled mango

1 tablespoon fresh lime juice

1 1/2 cups cubed peeled avocado (from 2 medium)

1/2 cup finely chopped red bell pepper

1/2 cup finely chopped red onion

1/4 cup finely chopped seeded jalapeño chiles (2 medium)

1/4 cup chopped fresh cilantro

1 cup shredded iceberg lettuce

1/2 teaspoon salt

Frances Pietsch | Flower Mound, TX

When it comes to comfort food, **Frances Pietsch** wants hers New Mexico style: a stack of red flat enchiladas topped with a fried egg and served with pinto beans and fried potatoes. Born and raised in New Mexico, Frances remembers all the cooking for Christmas. "My mom and aunts would get together and make dozens and dozens of tamales, taquitos and posole." Frances's kitchen features a seven-foot island "that makes cooking so much easier and enjoyable because I can lay everything out and have plenty of work space."

---

mango-jalapeño-chicken salad in cumin tortilla bowls

4 servings | Prep Time: **50 minutes** | Start to Finish: **50 minutes**

1 Heat oven to 400°F. Spray insides of 4 ovenproof 2-cup soup bowls with cooking spray.** Set aside.

2 In food processor bowl with metal blade or blender, place all vinaigrette ingredients except oil. Cover; process until smooth. With food processor running, slowly pour oil through feed tube until mixture is thickened. Set aside.

3 Spray 1 side of each tortilla with cooking spray. Sprinkle cumin and 1/2 teaspoon salt evenly over sprayed sides of tortillas. Press tortillas, seasoned sides up, in bowls. Place bowls in 15×10-inch pan. Bake 5 to 7 minutes or until edges are golden brown. Remove tortillas from bowls; place upside down on cooling rack. Cool completely.

4 In large bowl, mix chicken and remaining mango. In small bowl, mix 1 tablespoon lime juice and the avocado. Add avocado and remaining salad ingredients to chicken mixture; mix well. Add vinaigrette; mix well.

5 To serve, spoon chicken salad into tortilla bowls. (Bowls will be full.) Serve immediately.

*One large mango provides enough mango for both the vinaigrette and salad.

**Foil balls can be used instead of bowls. Cut 4 (25×12-inch) pieces of foil. Slightly crush each to make 4-inch ball; flatten slightly. Place on ungreased cookie sheet. Spray and season tortillas as directed; gently shape to fit over each foil ball, seasoned side toward foil. Bake as directed.

High Altitude (3500–6500 ft): No change.

1 Serving: Calories 740; Total Fat 40g (Saturated Fat 5g; Trans Fat 1g); Cholesterol 115mg; Sodium 1,000mg; Total Carbohydrate 48g (Dietary Fiber 6g) **Exchanges:** 1 Starch, 1 Fruit, 1 Other Carbohydrate, 6 Lean Meat, 4 1/2 Fat **Carbohydrate Choices:** 3

FILLING

1 package (17 oz) refrigerated fully cooked
   pork roast au jus
2 tablespoons orange juice
1/2 teaspoon ground cumin
1 medium tomato, chopped (3/4 cup)
1 medium avocado, pitted, peeled and
   chopped (3/4 cup)
2 teaspoons lime juice
1/2 teaspoon sugar
1/4 teaspoon salt

PESTO

1 1/2 cups lightly packed fresh cilantro sprigs
3/4 cup Spanish peanuts
2 to 3 cloves garlic
1 jalapeño chile, seeded, chopped
1/4 cup olive oil

TACO SHELLS AND CHEESE

1 box (4.7 oz) taco shells that stand on their
   own (10 shells)
1 cup shredded Monterey Jack cheese (4 oz)

GARNISHES, IF DESIRED

Lime and orange wedges
Fresh cilantro sprigs

Vanda Pozzanghera | Pittsford, NY

Vanda Pozzanghera
thought pork would make
a great main ingredient
for tacos. Prepackaged
roast pork would make it
simple to prepare. Vanda
is short on time but likes to experiment when she can. "It is rare that I
will follow a recipe—even my own—
to the letter. I take advantage of any
shortcuts I can. But I still try to provide
something more than just the stan-
dard." Vanda says being born in India
has influenced her cooking style. She
also has picked up ideas from friends
of many different cultural backgrounds.

category winner

mexican pesto-pork tacos

10 tacos I Prep Time: **40 minutes** I Start to Finish: **40 minutes**

1 Heat oven to 325°F. In medium microwavable bowl, shred pork;
discard juice. Toss pork with orange juice and cumin; set aside. In
another medium bowl, mix tomato, avocado, lime juice, sugar and
salt.

2 In food processor bowl with metal blade, place 1 1/2 cups cilantro,
the peanuts, garlic, chile and oil. Cover; process about 30 seconds
or until well blended; set aside.

3 Heat taco shells in oven as directed on box.

4 Meanwhile, cover bowl of pork mixture with microwavable paper
towel. Microwave on High 2 to 3 minutes or until warm.

5 To serve, spread about 1 tablespoon pesto over 1 side of each taco
shell. Fill each with about 1/4 cup warm pork mixture, 1 tablespoon
tomato-avocado mixture and heaping 1 tablespoon cheese. Serve
garnished with lime wedges, orange wedges and cilantro sprigs.

High Altitude (3500–6500 ft): No change.

1 Taco: Calories 390; Total Fat 28g (Saturated Fat 7g; Trans Fat 2g); Cholesterol 50mg; Sodium 320mg; Total Carbohydrate 13g (Dietary Fiber 3g) **Exchanges:** 1 Starch, 2 1/2 Lean Meat, 4 Fat **Carbohydrate Choices:** 1

2 large bell peppers (any color)

4 cups water

1 lb lean (at least 80%) ground beef

1 package (1 oz) taco seasoning mix

1 cup chunky-style salsa

1 can (16.3 oz) Pillsbury Grands! Homestyle refrigerated buttermilk biscuits (8 biscuits)

1 egg, slightly beaten

1 cup shredded Mexican cheese blend or Monterey Jack cheese (4 oz)

½ cup sour cream, if desired

Cynthia Bowser | Jonesborough, TN

Cynthia Bowser's cooking specialty is stuffed peppers and her baking specialty is cookies. Through experimenting, she's learned that a dash of salsa and taco mix adds a nice flavor boost—a trick she applied to this twist on stuffed peppers. Also high on her favorite food list: brown sugar–glazed ham at the holidays and her mother's meatloaf and mashed potatoes. Cynthia is excited about volunteering at one of the oldest fossil sites in the nation, the Gray Fossil Site in Tennessee.

mexican stuffed-pepper biscuit tostadas

8 servings | Prep Time: **30 minutes** | Start to Finish: **55 minutes**

1 Heat oven to 350°F. Lightly spray large cookie sheet with cooking spray.

2 Cut each bell pepper lengthwise into quarters, making 8 pieces; remove stems, seeds and membranes. In 2-quart saucepan, heat 4 cups water to boiling. Add bell pepper pieces; cook 5 minutes. Drain well on paper towels; set aside.

3 Meanwhile, in 10-inch skillet, cook beef over medium heat 8 to 10 minutes, stirring occasionally, until thoroughly cooked; drain. Stir in taco seasoning mix and salsa until well blended; set aside.

4 Separate dough into 8 biscuits. Place biscuits 2 inches apart on cookie sheet; brush with egg.

5 Press 1 pepper piece, skin side down, on each biscuit. Spoon heaping ¼ cup beef mixture into each pepper, spreading to cover pepper evenly. Sprinkle each with 2 tablespoons cheese.

6 Bake 18 to 22 minutes or until cheese is melted and edges of biscuits are golden brown. Cool 5 minutes. Top each with 1 tablespoon sour cream.

High Altitude (3500–6500 ft): In step 5, do not add cheese. In step 6, bake 20 minutes. Add cheese; bake 3 to 5 minutes longer or until cheese is melted.

1 Serving: Calories 370; Total Fat 19g (Saturated Fat 8g; Trans Fat 4g); Cholesterol 70mg; Sodium 1,380mg; Total Carbohydrate 31g (Dietary Fiber 1g) Exchanges: 1½ Starch, ½ Other Carbohydrate, 2 High-Fat Meat, ½ Fat Carbohydrate Choices: 2

SAUCE

2 cans (10 oz each) mild enchilada sauce
1/2 cup creamy peanut butter
1/2 teaspoon sugar
1/2 teaspoon ground cinnamon
1/2 oz bittersweet baking chocolate

ENCHILADAS

1 1/2 cups shredded mild white Cheddar and
  Monterey Jack cheese blend or Cheddar-
  Monterey Jack cheese blend*
1 package (11.5 oz) flour tortillas for burritos
  (8 tortillas)
2 cups cooked chicken breast strips
  (2 1/4 × 1/4 inch)
1/4 cup cocktail peanuts, chopped
1 teaspoon lime juice
1 container (8 oz) sour cream
2 tablespoons chopped fresh cilantro

Margaret Martinez |
Westminster, CO

"I've loved mole forever and order it whenever I see it on a menu," says **Margaret Martinez**. Mole is widely regarded as the national dish of Mexico, but making it from scratch is too much trouble, she adds. Her recipe provides an easy way to enjoy it, one that's fast enough for a "working mom." Plus, it's a great way to use up leftover chicken or turkey, Margaret says. Her new career is that of ski instructor. "I love teaching people to ski and love seeing families enjoy the sport together."

peanut butter mole enchiladas

8 servings | Prep Time: **20 minutes** | Start to Finish: **50 minutes**

1 Heat oven to 325°F. In 2-quart saucepan, cook enchilada sauce over medium-low heat about 5 minutes, stirring occasionally, until heated. Stir in peanut butter and sugar; cook 1 to 2 minutes or until peanut butter is melted. Remove from heat. Add cinnamon and chocolate; stir until chocolate is melted.

2 Spray 13×9-inch (3-quart) glass baking dish with cooking spray. Spoon about 1/2 cup sauce over bottom of baking dish. Reserve 1/2 cup cheese. Fill each tortilla with about 1/4 cup chicken, 2 tablespoons cheese and heaping 1 tablespoon sauce. Roll up tortillas; place seam sides down in baking dish. Pour remaining sauce evenly over tortillas.

3 Cover loosely with foil; bake 25 to 30 minutes or until thoroughly heated.

4 Sprinkle with reserved 1/2 cup cheese. Bake uncovered 2 to 3 minutes longer or until cheese is melted. Sprinkle with peanuts.

5 In small bowl, stir lime juice into sour cream until mixed. Top individual servings with sour cream mixture and cilantro.

* 3/4 cup shredded mild white Cheddar cheese and 3/4 cup Monterey Jack cheese can be used instead of the cheese blend.

High Altitude (3500–6500 ft): Heat oven to 350°F.

1 Serving: Calories 500; Total Fat 31g (Saturated Fat 12g; Trans Fat 2g); Cholesterol 70mg; Sodium 930mg; Total Carbohydrate 31g (Dietary Fiber 1g) **Exchanges:** 1 1/2 Starch, 1/2 Other Carbohydrate, 3 High-Fat Meat, 1 Fat **Carbohydrate Choices:** 2

1 1/2 lb beef flank steak
1 package (1 oz) taco seasoning mix
6 tablespoons butter or margarine, melted
1 clove garlic, finely chopped
1 1/2 teaspoons fresh lime juice
1/4 cup water
2 cans (11 oz each) Pillsbury refrigerated crusty French loaf
1/2 teaspoon garlic powder
2 tablespoons canola oil
1 medium onion, thinly sliced
1 medium green bell pepper, thinly sliced
1 medium red bell pepper, thinly sliced
1/4 cup finely chopped fresh cilantro, if desired
1 jar (8 oz) cheese dip
1 can (4.5 oz) chopped green chiles

Tena Kerns | **Berkley, MA**

Tena Kerns's recipe gives familiar Philly Cheese Steak a twist. When she served it to her family, even her "picky children" ate it, she says. Tena learned to cook by helping her Korean mother. Her favorite family meal is her mother's Korean food: marinated beef ribs, fried rice and egg rolls. All 17 members of Tena's extended family traveled to Las Vegas in 2006. "Being with my entire family on vacation was a true blessing," she says. The best cooking tip she received was from her mom: Never make a new recipe to bring to a party.

philly-goes-mexican cheese steak

4 sandwiches | Prep Time: **40 minutes** | Start to Finish: **1 hour**

1 Heat oven to 350°F. Spray large cookie sheet with cooking spray. Cut beef steak against the grain into thin strips; set aside. Reserve 2 teaspoons of the taco seasoning mix.

2 In large bowl, mix 3 tablespoons of the butter, remaining taco seasoning mix, garlic, lime juice and water. Add beef; toss to coat. Refrigerate beef mixture while baking bread.

3 Place bread loaves, at least 2 inches apart, on cookie sheet. With sharp knife, make slits on top of each loaf. In small bowl, stir remaining 3 tablespoons butter, reserved 2 teaspoons taco seasoning mix and the garlic powder until well mixed. Brush seasoning mixture on tops and sides of each loaf. Bake 26 to 30 minutes or until golden brown. Cool 15 minutes.

4 Meanwhile, in 12-inch nonstick skillet, heat 1 tablespoon of the oil over medium-high heat. Add onion and bell peppers; cook 6 to 8 minutes, stirring frequently, until vegetables are tender. Remove vegetables from skillet; set aside.

5 In same skillet, heat remaining 1 tablespoon oil over high heat. Add half of the beef; cook 8 to 10 minutes, stirring frequently, until tender and browned. Transfer cooked beef to a plate; cook remaining half of beef. Return beef and vegetables to skillet. Stir in cilantro. Keep warm.

6 In small microwavable bowl, stir cheese dip and chiles. Cover with microwavable plastic wrap, folding back one edge 1/4 inch to vent steam. Microwave on High 3 minutes, stirring after 1 minute 30 seconds, until warm.

7 Cut each bread loaf in half crosswise, then cut each half horizontally ¾ of the way through. To serve, fill each roll with ¼ of the beef mixture; drizzle with cheese sauce. Serve immediately.

High Altitude (3500–6500 ft): No change.

1 Sandwich: Calories 1,000; Total Fat 43g (Saturated Fat 19g; Trans Fat 2g); Cholesterol 190mg; Sodium 2,610mg; Total Carbohydrate 86g (Dietary Fiber 3g) **Exchanges:** 4 Starch, 1½ Other Carbohydrate, 1 Vegetable, 7 Lean Meat, 4 Fat **Carbohydrate Choices:** 6

1/4 cup canola oil
1 small onion, chopped (1/4 cup)
1 clove garlic, finely chopped
1 lb lean (at least 80%) ground beef
1 large tomato, chopped (1 cup)
1 can (4.5 oz) chopped green chiles
1 package (1 oz) taco seasoning mix
1/2 cup cinnamon applesauce or plain
   applesauce
1/4 cup raisins
1/3 cup sliced almonds
1/2 cup pimiento-stuffed green olives,
   coarsely chopped
1 package (11.5 oz) flour tortillas for burritos
   (8 tortillas)
1 cup sour cream
4 medium green onions, chopped (1/4 cup)
1/4 cup chopped fresh cilantro

picadillo chimichangas

8 servings | Prep Time: **35 minutes** | Start to Finish: **50 minutes**

1 Heat oven to 475°F. Brush large cookie sheet with 1 tablespoon of the oil.

2 In 10-inch skillet, heat 2 tablespoons of the oil over medium heat. Add onion and garlic; cook 1 to 2 minutes, stirring occasionally, until onion is tender. Stir in beef; cook 8 to 10 minutes, stirring occasionally, until beef is thoroughly cooked; drain.

3 Reduce heat to medium-low. Stir in tomato, chiles, taco seasoning mix, applesauce and raisins; cook 10 minutes, stirring occasionally. Stir in almonds and olives; cook 1 to 2 minutes or until thoroughly heated.

4 For each chimichanga, spoon 1/2 cup beef mixture down center of each tortilla. Fold sides of each tortilla toward center; fold ends up. Place seam sides down on cookie sheet. Brush tops and sides of chimichangas with remaining 1 tablespoon oil.

5 Bake 6 to 8 minutes or until golden brown. Cool on cookie sheet 5 minutes.

6 Meanwhile, in small bowl, stir sour cream, green onions and 2 tablespoons of the cilantro.

7 To serve, top each chimichanga with 2 tablespoons sour cream mixture and remaining cilantro.

High Altitude (3500–6500 ft): Bake 10 to 12 minutes.

1 **Serving:** Calories 420; Total Fat 26g (Saturated Fat 8g; Trans Fat 2g); Cholesterol 55mg; Sodium 950mg; Total Carbohydrate 32g (Dietary Fiber 2g) **Exchanges:** 1 1/2 Starch, 1/2 Other Carbohydrate, 1 1/2 Medium-Fat Meat, 3 1/2 Fat **Carbohydrate Choices:** 2

Sherry Roper | San Diego, CA

Sherry Roper researched many recipes for chimichangas and picadillo. She designed her version to be easier and quicker than many others, without sacrificing taste. For example, Sherry's recipe includes prepared ingredients and her chimichangas are baked (instead of deep fried). Sherry recently sold two of her watercolor paintings and won an honorable mention in a local art show. Few recipes intimidate Sherry. She simply heeds her mom's advice: "Just follow the directions!"

5 fresh poblano chiles (4 1/2 × 3 inch)

1 1/2 cups shredded Chihuahua or Monterey Jack cheese (6 oz)

1 cup shredded Mexican cheese blend (4 oz)

1/3 cup ricotta cheese

2 cloves garlic, finely chopped

1/2 teaspoon ground cumin

1 box (9 oz) frozen spinach, thawed, squeezed to drain

1 can (12 oz) Pillsbury Golden Layers Butter Tastin' refrigerated biscuits (10 biscuits)

1 can (10 oz) mild enchilada sauce

2 plum (Roma) tomatoes, chopped, if desired

1/2 cup fresh guacamole, if desired

1/2 cup sour cream, if desired

Gloria Felts | Indianapolis, IN

Gloria Felts always loved to cook, and even more so after she became a vegetarian as a teenager. Her new diet drove her to learn about different cuisines and ingredients. Today, Gloria enjoys enhancing flavors with poblano chiles, and with this recipe she succeeded in finding a creative use for them. Gloria says that cooks unfamiliar with peppers may be intimidated by the thought of roasting and peeling them, but it's quite easy and actually fun to do—just be sure to wear gloves. Gloria collects hard-to-find brown glasses and dishes.

poblanos florentine casserole

9 servings | Prep Time: **45 minutes** | Start to Finish: **2 hours 5 minutes**

1 Set oven control to broil. On cookie sheet, broil chiles with tops 2 inches from heat about 10 minutes, turning frequently with tongs, until all sides are blackened and blistered. Place chiles in paper bag; seal bag. Let chiles steam 15 minutes.

2 Heat oven to 350°F. Lightly spray 8-inch square (2-quart) glass baking dish with cooking spray.

3 In medium bowl, mix Chihuahua cheese and Mexican cheese blend; reserve 3/4 cup for topping. In another medium bowl, mix ricotta cheese, garlic, cumin and spinach. Stir in remaining shredded cheeses. Set aside.

4 Wearing food-safe plastic gloves, peel blackened skin from chiles. Cut open chiles; remove stems, seeds and membranes. Cut each chile in half lengthwise into 2 pieces; pat dry.

5 Separate dough into 10 biscuits. Separate each biscuit into 2 thin layers; flatten slightly.

6 Pour half of the enchilada sauce over bottom of baking dish. Place 10 biscuit layers on sauce, cutting biscuits if necessary to fit into dish. Top with 5 chile halves; spread spinach mixture over chiles. Top with remaining 5 chile halves and remaining 10 biscuit layers. Pour remaining enchilada sauce over biscuits.

7 Spray sheet of foil with cooking spray. Cover baking dish with foil, sprayed side down. Bake 55 to 60 minutes or until thoroughly heated and bubbly around edges.

8 Sprinkle with reserved 3/4 cup shredded cheeses. Bake uncovered 5 to 8 minutes longer or until cheese is melted. Cool 10 minutes before cutting. Top each serving with tomatoes, guacamole and sour cream.

High Altitude (3500–6500 ft): No change.

1 Serving: Calories 290; Total Fat 16g (Saturated Fat 8g; Trans Fat 2g); Cholesterol 30mg; Sodium 790mg; Total Carbohydrate 23g (Dietary Fiber 1g) **Exchanges:** 1 Starch, 1/2 Other Carbohydrate, 1 High-Fat Meat, 1 1/2 Fat **Carbohydrate Choices:** 1 1/2

SAUCE

1 box (10 oz) frozen corn and butter sauce

1 can (4.5 oz) chopped green chiles

1 tablespoon sugar

1/4 cup lightly packed fresh cilantro sprigs

3/4 cup milk

ENCHILADAS

1 tablespoon light olive oil

1 teaspoon lime juice

12 oz uncooked medium shrimp (about 24),
    thawed if frozen, peeled and deveined

1/2 teaspoon ground cumin

1 cup refrigerated cooked shredded hash
    brown potatoes (from 20-oz bag)

1/4 cup diced red bell pepper

1 jalapeño chile, seeded, diced

2 cups shredded Mexican cheese blend (8 oz)

8 flour tortillas for soft tacos and fajitas
    (from 10.5-oz package)

Finely shredded red cabbage, if desired

Finely chopped green onions, if desired

Barbara Hahn | Park Hills, MO

Barbara Hahn grew up in Texas where she developed an appetite for Mexican cuisine like her shrimp enchiladas, adapted from an entrée she sampled at a restaurant. Her version features a bed of slightly sweet and creamy corn sauce, enlivened with green chiles and cilantro. Barbara lives on a 1,200-acre farm, where her sons are starting a winery. One of her proudest accomplishments was returning to college as an older adult and graduating. She often has an audience when she cooks: friends, family and three dachshunds underfoot.

shrimp enchiladas with sweet corn sauce

4 servings | Prep Time: **35 minutes** | Start to Finish: **1 hour 5 minutes**

1 Heat oven to 350°F. Spray 13×9-inch (3-quart) glass baking dish with cooking spray.

2 Cook corn in microwave as directed on package.

3 In blender or food processor, place 1 cup of the corn and butter sauce, 3 tablespoons of the green chiles, the sugar, cilantro and milk. Cover; blend on medium speed until creamy. Pour into medium bowl; stir in remaining corn and butter sauce until well mixed. Set aside.

4 In 10-inch nonstick skillet, heat oil and lime juice over medium-high heat. Add shrimp; sprinkle cumin over shrimp. Cook 2 to 3 minutes, turning once, until shrimp are pink. Remove shrimp from skillet to cutting board; chop. Set aside.

5 In same skillet, cook potatoes over medium heat 4 to 5 minutes, turning occasionally, until thoroughly heated. Remove from heat. Stir in shrimp, remaining green chiles, the bell pepper, jalapeño chile and cheese until mixed.

6 Heat tortillas in microwave as directed on package.

7 Pour half of the corn sauce in bottom of baking dish. Spoon about 1/2 cup shrimp mixture down center of each tortilla. Roll up each tortilla; place seam side down on corn sauce in baking dish. Pour remaining corn sauce evenly over enchiladas.

8 Bake 25 to 30 minutes or until thoroughly heated. To serve, place 2 enchiladas on each of 4 serving plates. Garnish with cabbage and onions.

High Altitude (3500–6500 ft): Heat oven to 375°F.

1 Serving (2 enchiladas each): Calories 630; Total Fat 29g (Saturated Fat 14g; Trans Fat 2g); Cholesterol 175mg; Sodium 1,310mg; Total Carbohydrate 59g (Dietary Fiber 4g) **Exchanges:** 3 Starch, 1 Other Carbohydrate, 3 1/2 Lean Meat, 3 Fat **Carbohydrate Choices:** 4

1 container (8 oz) chives-and-onion cream cheese spread

¾ teaspoon garlic powder

⅓ cup drained pickled jalapeño slices (from 12-oz jar)

½ cup canned (drained) whole kernel corn

6 taco shells (from 4.6-oz box), coarsely broken

¾ teaspoon chili powder

4 boneless skinless chicken breasts (about 1¼ lb)

2 tablespoons butter or margarine, melted

½ to ¾ cup buttermilk

3 tablespoons honey

1 cup shredded Mexican cheese blend (4 oz)

1⅔ cups chunky-style salsa

⅔ cup sour cream

Deborah Puette | Lilburn, GA

This chicken is moist on the inside and crunchy on the outside, thanks to the creative use of taco shells as crust in her recipe, says **Deborah Puette**. The jalapeños add a kick and the honey adds contrast. Deborah has followed the Bake-Off® Contest since she was 12 and loves reading about its history. Her family gets a new dish at least once a week. "I love to cook fast and easy on weekdays and elaborate on weekends," she says. She needs to visit just one more state to reach her goal of visiting all 50.

---

southwestern cheese-stuffed chicken roll-ups

4 servings | Prep Time: **30 minutes** | Start to Finish: **1 hour 20 minutes**

1 Heat oven to 350°F. In medium bowl, stir together cream cheese, garlic powder, jalapeños and corn; set aside.

2 In resealable food-storage plastic bag, place broken taco shells; seal bag. Crush taco shells with rolling pin until coarsely ground. (Or, place broken taco shells in food processor bowl with metal blade; process until coarsely ground.) Pour crumbs into shallow dish; stir in chili powder.

3 Between pieces of plastic wrap or waxed paper, place each chicken breast, smooth side down; gently pound with flat side of meat mallet or rolling pin until about ¼ inch thick. Spread butter over one side of each chicken breast.

4 Place about ⅓ cup cream cheese mixture on center of buttered side of each chicken breast; roll up chicken. Pour buttermilk into shallow dish. Dip chicken rolls in buttermilk, then coat with crumb mixture. Insert toothpick to secure. Place in ungreased 8-inch square (2-quart) glass baking dish. Drizzle with honey.

5 Bake 35 to 45 minutes or until chicken is no longer pink in center. Sprinkle with Mexican cheese blend; bake 4 to 5 minutes longer until cheese is melted. Serve with salsa and sour cream.

High Altitude (3500–6500 ft): Heat oven to 375°F.

1 Serving: Calories 780; Total Fat 47g (Saturated Fat 26g; Trans Fat 3g); Cholesterol 205mg; Sodium 1,720mg; Total Carbohydrate 44g (Dietary Fiber 1g) **Exchanges:** 1½ Starch, 1½ Other Carbohydrate, 5½ Lean Meat, 6 Fat **Carbohydrate Choices:** 3

2 tablespoons blackened seasoning (from 2.5-oz container)

1 tablespoon olive oil

1/4 cup orange marmalade

1 lb uncooked medium shrimp (about 32), thawed if frozen, peeled and deveined, tails removed

2 ripe medium avocados, pitted, peeled and cut into 1/2-inch pieces

1 small orange, peeled, chopped

1 small jalapeño chile, seeded, finely chopped

1/4 cup chopped red onion

2 tablespoons chopped fresh cilantro

1 can (15 oz) black beans, drained, rinsed

1 teaspoon ground cumin

1 tablespoon fresh lime juice

8 taco shells that stand on their own (from 4.7-oz box)

2 cups shredded Cheddar–Monterey Jack cheese blend (8 oz)

Karen Gulkin | Simpsonville, SC

Karen Gulkin's taco recipe earned raves from her entire family. She says it's beautiful, delicious and "has a variety of fresh Mexican flavors that are fantastic." Karen recently visited Provence, France, where she stayed at a chef's guesthouse. During the day, the popular chef gave tours of local villages, sharing his wealth of historical knowledge. Each evening the group gathered in his kitchen for instruction, preparing a fabulous meal. Karen enjoys watching hummingbirds feed just outside her kitchen window.

spicy citrus shrimp and black bean tacos with orange-avocado salsa

4 servings | Prep Time: **45 minutes** | Start to Finish: **45 minutes**

1 Reserve 1 teaspoon of the blackened seasoning. In large resealable food-storage plastic bag, place oil, marmalade and remaining blackened seasoning; seal bag and shake. Add shrimp; seal bag and mix well. Refrigerate at least 30 minutes but no longer than 24 hours.

2 Meanwhile, in medium bowl, gently toss avocados, orange, chile, onion and cilantro until mixed. Cover; set aside.

3 In food processor bowl with metal blade, place reserved 1 teaspoon blackened seasoning, the black beans, cumin and lime juice. Cover; process with on-and-off pulses until mixed and beans are coarsely chopped.

4 Heat oven to 350°F. Place taco shells on cookie sheet. Divide bean mixture evenly among shells. Sprinkle with cheese. Bake 6 to 8 minutes or until cheese is melted.

5 Meanwhile, spray large skillet with cooking spray; heat over medium-high heat. Add shrimp; cook 3 to 5 minutes, turning once, until pink. Remove taco shells from oven; place 4 cooked shrimp in each shell. Top with avocado salsa.

High Altitude (3500–6500 ft): No change.

1 Serving (2 tacos each): Calories 830; Total Fat 43g (Saturated Fat 16g; Trans Fat 3g); Cholesterol 220mg; Sodium 950mg; Total Carbohydrate 68g (Dietary Fiber 18g) **Exchanges:** 3 Starch, 1 1/2 Other Carbohydrate, 5 Lean Meat, 5 Fat **Carbohydrate Choices:** 4 1/2

BURRITOS

$^1/_2$ cup uncooked regular long-grain white rice

1 cup water

1 small onion, finely chopped ($^1/_4$ cup)

2 cloves garlic, finely chopped

2 teaspoons chili powder

1 teaspoon ground cumin

$^1/_4$ teaspoon ground cinnamon

$^1/_2$ teaspoon salt

1 chipotle chile in adobo sauce, finely chopped

2 tablespoons apricot preserves

2 tablespoons chopped green chiles (from 4.5-oz can)

$^1/_4$ cup raisins

2 teaspoons unsweetened baking cocoa

2 tablespoons finely ground almonds

1 lb lean ground pork

$^1/_2$ cup reduced-sodium chicken broth

1 can (10 oz) mild enchilada sauce

1 can (15 oz) pinto beans, drained, rinsed

14 flour tortillas for burritos (from two 11.5-oz packages)

2 cups shredded sharp Cheddar cheese (8 oz)

GARNISHES

$1^1/_2$ cups sour cream

Cilantro sprigs

Mike Briggs | **Arlington, VA**

Mike Briggs and his fiancée share an interest in cooking, and they've learned to navigate his narrow, galley-style kitchen "without major collision or injury," he says. She "gently but unequivocally" led him to believe that the future of their relationship depended on his entering this recipe in the Bake-Off® Contest. Mike tried his hand at making a Mexican mole after enjoying an enchilada in a Texas restaurant. He discovered it was complicated and decided to create a simpler version with the same great taste.

spicy mole pork burritos

14 servings | Prep Time: **35 minutes** | Start to Finish: **1 hour 5 minutes**

1 Cook rice in water as directed on package. Meanwhile, in small bowl, mix onion, garlic, chili powder, cumin, cinnamon and salt; set aside. In another small bowl, mix chipotle chile, preserves, green chiles, raisins, cocoa and almonds; set aside.

2 In 12-inch skillet, cook pork over medium-high heat 8 to 10 minutes, stirring occasionally, until no longer pink; drain.

3 Stir onion mixture into pork; cook over medium heat 2 minutes, stirring occasionally. Stir in preserves mixture, broth and enchilada sauce; heat to boiling. Reduce heat to low. Simmer uncovered 30 minutes, stirring occasionally. Stir in beans and rice; cook 2 to 3 minutes or until hot and bubbly.

4 Meanwhile, heat tortillas as directed on package. To assemble, spoon slightly less than $^1/_2$ cup pork filling down center of each tortilla. Sprinkle about 1 tablespoon cheese over filling on each. Fold in ends of each tortilla; fold sides toward center, overlapping edges.

5 To serve, place burritos, folded sides down, on plates. Garnish each serving with about 1 tablespoon sour cream and cilantro sprigs. Serve with tortilla chips, if desired.

High Altitude (3500–6500 ft): No change.

1 Serving: Calories 410; Total Fat 20g (Saturated Fat 9g; Trans Fat 2g); Cholesterol 55mg; Sodium 740mg; Total Carbohydrate 41g (Dietary Fiber 3g) Exchanges: 2 Starch, $^1/_2$ Other Carbohydrate, $1^1/_2$ Lean Meat, 3 Fat Carbohydrate Choices: 3

1 can (10 oz) mild enchilada sauce

1 cup crema Mexicana table cream or sour cream

1 tablespoon olive oil

1 medium onion, chopped ($\frac{1}{2}$ cup)

3 cloves garlic, finely chopped

1 package (8 oz) sliced fresh baby portabella mushrooms

1 box (9 oz) frozen spinach, thawed, squeezed to drain

$\frac{1}{3}$ cup chopped drained roasted red bell peppers (from 7.25-oz jar)

2 tablespoons taco seasoning mix (from 1-oz package)

$\frac{1}{4}$ cup lightly packed fresh cilantro sprigs

$\frac{1}{2}$ teaspoon ground cumin

1$\frac{1}{4}$ cups shredded pepper Jack or salsa Jack cheese (5 oz)

2 cups shredded quesadilla or mozzarella cheese (8 oz)

10 flour tortillas for soft tacos and fajitas (from 10.5-oz package)

$\frac{1}{2}$ cup crumbled cotija cheese or fresh mozzarella cheese

Robin Hill | Arlington, TX

Robin Hill grew up cooking and eating Tex-Mex food, so it wasn't a stretch for her to create these vegetarian enchiladas. She's successfully filled ravioli and empanadas with spinach and mushrooms, and thought it would work in enchiladas, too. Her husband's positive reaction, and subsequent rave reviews from others, clinched her decision to enter the Bake-Off® Contest. One of her family's holiday traditions is to make Robin's famous baked lemon soufflé. They use an old copper bowl to beat the egg whites, and everyone takes a turn.

spinach and mushroom enchiladas with creamy red sauce

5 servings | Prep Time: **45 minutes** | Start to Finish: **1 hour 25 minutes**

1 Heat oven to 350°F. Spray 13×9-inch (3-quart) glass baking dish with cooking spray.

2 In 1-quart saucepan, heat enchilada sauce and $\frac{1}{2}$ cup of the crema Mexicana over medium heat 2 to 3 minutes, stirring occasionally, until warm. Spread $\frac{1}{4}$ cup of the sauce mixture on bottom of baking dish. Set aside remaining sauce.

3 In 12-inch nonstick skillet, heat oil over medium-high heat. Add onion and garlic; cook 2 to 3 minutes, stirring occasionally, until onion is tender. Stir in mushrooms; cook 7 to 8 minutes, stirring occasionally, until mushrooms are tender.

4 Transfer vegetable mixture to food processor bowl with metal blade. Add spinach, roasted peppers, taco seasoning mix, 2 tablespoons of the cilantro, the cumin and remaining $\frac{1}{2}$ cup crema Mexicana. Cover; process with on-and-off pulses 6 to 8 times or until mushrooms are coarsely chopped. Pour mixture into large bowl; stir in pepper Jack cheese and 1$\frac{1}{4}$ cups of the quesadilla cheese.

5 Spoon $\frac{1}{3}$ cup vegetable filling down center of each tortilla. Roll up tortillas; place seam sides down on sauce in baking dish. Pour remaining sauce evenly over tortillas; sprinkle with remaining $\frac{3}{4}$ cup quesadilla cheese and the cotija cheese. Spray sheet of foil with cooking spray; cover baking dish tightly with foil, sprayed side down.

6 Bake 35 to 40 minutes or until thoroughly heated. Chop remaining 2 tablespoons cilantro; sprinkle over enchiladas before serving.

High Altitude (3500–6500 ft): Heat oven to 375°F.

1 Serving (2 enchiladas each): Calories 660; Total Fat 43g (Saturated Fat 23g; Trans Fat 2g); Cholesterol 110mg; Sodium 1,660mg; Total Carbohydrate 41g (Dietary Fiber 3g) **Exchanges:** 2 Starch, $\frac{1}{2}$ Other Carbohydrate, 1 Vegetable, 3 High-Fat Meat, 3 Fat **Carbohydrate Choices:** 3

1/2 cup uncooked basmati rice, rinsed

1 cup water

1 cup medium chunky-style salsa

1/3 cup crunchy peanut butter

2 tablespoons teriyaki sauce

2 tablespoons water

1/4 cup packed light brown sugar

1 teaspoon chili powder

1/2 teaspoon ground ginger

1 lb boneless skinless chicken breasts, cut into bite-size pieces

2 teaspoons sesame oil

6 flour tortillas for burritos (from 11.5-oz package)

6 tablespoons medium chunky-style salsa

6 tablespoons sour cream

Sharon Koebel | Loveland, OH

Peanut butter rates as **Sharon Koebel**'s favorite ingredient and is part of her finalist recipe. Her burritos blend Mexican and Asian foods—soft, crunchy, spicy and sweet—into one easy-to-prepare recipe, she says. Sharon cherishes her memories of watching her grandmother cook. "She's the one that taught me to improvise and cook by adding a 'pinch' of this and a 'handful' of that." Sharon's favorite part of her job is interacting with patients, families and fellow employees. "No two days are ever the same," she says.

thai chicken burritos

6 burritos | Prep Time: **45 minutes** | Start to Finish: **45 minutes**

1 Cook rice in water as directed on package, omitting butter, if called for.

2 Meanwhile, in small bowl, mix 1 cup salsa, the peanut butter, teriyaki sauce, water and brown sugar; set aside.

3 In large resealable food-storage plastic bag, mix chili powder and ginger. Add chicken; seal bag and shake until chicken is evenly coated.

4 In 10-inch nonstick skillet, heat oil over medium-high heat. Add chicken; cook 3 to 5 minutes, stirring frequently, until chicken is no longer pink in center. Stir in salsa mixture. Reduce heat to low. Cover; simmer 8 to 10 minutes. Stir in cooked rice; cook 2 to 3 minutes longer or until mixture is thoroughly heated.

5 Meanwhile, heat tortillas as directed on package. Spoon 1/2 cup chicken filling down center of each warm tortilla to within 1 inch of edge of tortilla. Fold sides of tortilla toward center; fold ends over. Place burritos, folded sides down, on serving plate. Top each with 1 tablespoon salsa and 1 tablespoon sour cream.

High Altitude (3500–6500 ft): No change.

1 Burrito: Calories 470; Total Fat 18g (Saturated Fat 5g; Trans Fat 1g); Cholesterol 55mg; Sodium 1,250mg; Total Carbohydrate 52g (Dietary Fiber 1g) Exchanges: 2 Starch, 1 1/2 Other Carbohydrate, 2 1/2 Lean Meat, 2 Fat Carbohydrate Choices: 3 1/2

1³/₄ lb boneless skinless chicken breasts

1 tablespoon peanut oil

1 package (1 oz) 40% less-sodium taco seasoning mix

¹/₂ cup bottled peanut sauce

1 teaspoon red curry paste

2 tablespoons fresh lime juice

2 tablespoons sugar

1 package (11.5 oz) flour tortillas for burritos (8 tortillas)

¹/₂ cup sour cream

2 cups shredded Monterey Jack cheese (8 oz)

2²/₃ cups finely shredded lettuce

¹/₂ cup very thinly sliced red onion

Decorative toothpicks, if desired

Sarah Lafon | Franklin, TN

Sarah Lafon describes herself as a singer/song-writer, but says she "has had little time to pursue my music career lately with two little ones to chase around." Sarah has produced a CD, and she and her husband recently launched a website. A self-proclaimed kitchen experimenter, Sarah says, "I can hardly make a recipe as printed. I have to 'tinker' with it and make at least a change or two." She says the two most popular foods she makes are her lasagna and peanut-butter cheesecake.

thai-style mexican chicken wraps

8 servings | Prep Time: **35 minutes** | Start to Finish: **35 minutes**

1 Cut chicken into small bite-size pieces. In 12-inch nonstick skillet, heat oil over medium-high heat until hot. Add chicken; sprinkle with taco seasoning mix. Cook 5 to 7 minutes, stirring frequently, until chicken is no longer pink in center. Remove from heat; cover to keep warm.

2 Meanwhile, in small microwavable bowl, mix peanut sauce, red curry paste, lime juice and sugar. Microwave uncovered on High 30 to 40 seconds or until warm. Stir thoroughly until all of the curry paste is dissolved.

3 Heat tortillas by placing one at a time in 10-inch nonstick skillet or on hot nonstick griddle on medium-high heat 3 to 5 seconds, turning once.

4 To assemble each wrap, spoon about ¹/₂ cup chicken mixture down center of 1 tortilla. Top with sour cream, cheese, lettuce and onion. Drizzle with generous 1 tablespoon curry-peanut sauce. Fold 2 sides of tortilla to the middle; secure with toothpick. Serve warm.

High Altitude (3500–6500 ft): No change.

1 Serving: Calories 470; Total Fat 24g (Saturated Fat 10g; Trans Fat 2g); Cholesterol 95mg; Sodium 810mg; Total Carbohydrate 30g (Dietary Fiber 0g) **Exchanges:** 1 Starch, 1 Other Carbohydrate, 4¹/₂ Lean Meat, 2 Fat **Carbohydrate Choices:** 2

Niki Plourde, Gardner, Massachusetts, received $5,000 and a brand new range for her Apple-Jack Chicken Pizza with Caramelized Onions (p. 142). Judges declared her winning pizza a well-rounded, great family meal.

chapter four

pizza creations

Enjoy these fresh new pizza ideas or panini sandwiches for casual meals or hearty snacks.

Trends in Pizza Creations Category

Favorite flavor profiles—from appetizers to main dishes—were turned into pizzas. Among the most creative were: salad pizzas as seen on restaurant menus, a hot dog pizza featuring all the favorite condiments, a chicken Marsala pizza and a loaded baked potato pizza.

Red tomato sauce has been replaced by a variety of sauces, including Alfredo, mole, hummus and barbecue.

Fresh fruit was a frequent pizza topping, both on dessert and savory pizzas. Cooks topped pizzas with chopped apples, mango and honeydew.

Nuts were sprinkled extensively on pizzas, including almonds, pecans, peanuts, cashews and walnuts. Some of the flavor combinations with walnuts were ham, avocado and pesto; apples and tomato slices; and beef tenderloin, spinach and blue cheese.

Flavor was added to pizza crusts by brushing the crusts with oil or melted butter and adding herbs, spices or seeds, or mixing melted butter or oil with pesto or teriyaki sauce or seasoning mixes, such as taco or chimichurri seasoning.

1 can (13.8 oz) Pillsbury refrigerated classic pizza crust

4 teaspoons basil pesto

1/4 cup Caesar dressing (creamy or vinaigrette style)

8 oz water-packed fresh mozzarella cheese, drained and cut into 8 slices, or 8 slices (1 oz each) regular mozzarella cheese

1/4 teaspoon freshly ground pepper

12 slices cooked bacon

2 plum (Roma) tomatoes, each cut into 4 slices

8 large fresh basil leaves

1/4 cup butter or margarine

bacon, caesar and mozzarella panini

4 sandwiches | Prep Time: **40 minutes** | Start to Finish: **50 minutes**

1 Heat oven to 375°F. Spray large cookie sheet with cooking spray. Unroll pizza crust dough on cookie sheet; press dough into 16×11-inch rectangle, pulling dough gently if necessary. Bake 9 to 16 minutes or until light brown. Cool about 15 minutes or until cool enough to handle.

2 Cut cooled pizza crust in half lengthwise and crosswise to make 4 rectangles. Remove rectangles from cookie sheet; cut each rectangle in half crosswise for a total of 8 squares.

3 On each of 4 crust slices, spread 1 teaspoon pesto; set aside. On each of remaining 4 slices, spread 1 tablespoon Caesar dressing. Place 2 cheese slices on each crust slice with Caesar dressing. Top cheese with pepper, 3 bacon slices, 2 tomato slices and 2 basil leaves. Top with remaining crust slices, pesto sides down.

4 Heat 12-inch skillet or cast-iron skillet over medium heat until hot. Melt 2 tablespoons of the butter in skillet. Place 2 sandwiches in skillet. Place smaller skillet or saucepan on sandwiches to flatten slightly; keep skillet on sandwiches while cooking. Cook 1 to 2 minutes on each side or until bread is golden brown and crisp and fillings are heated. Remove from skillet; cover with foil to keep warm. Repeat with remaining 2 tablespoons butter and sandwiches.

High Altitude (3500–6500 ft): No change.

1 Sandwich: Calories 760; Total Fat 47g (Saturated Fat 20g; Trans Fat 1g); Cholesterol 90mg; Sodium 1,840mg; Total Carbohydrate 51g (Dietary Fiber 0g) Exchanges: 2 1/2 Starch, 1 Other Carbohydrate, 3 1/2 High-Fat Meat, 3 1/2 Fat Carbohydrate Choices: 3 1/2

Carole Strachan | Houston, TX

"All you need are two skillets, fresh ingredients and Pillsbury refrigerated pizza crust to get a hot gourmet sandwich straight from your kitchen to your table," says **Carole Strachan**. The fresh ingredients include basil, mozzarella and tomatoes. Carole, her husband and friends have made three trips to the British Virgin Islands, where they charter a 50-foot catamaran and go island hopping. Her home has a 1,200-square-foot deck built around a huge oak tree. "It's great for entertaining," says Carole, who enjoys grilling.

3 tablespoons butter or margarine

2 large sweet onions (such as Maui or Walla Walla), very thinly sliced

$\frac{1}{2}$ teaspoon dried thyme leaves

$\frac{1}{8}$ teaspoon salt

$\frac{1}{8}$ teaspoon pepper

1 can (13.8 oz) Pillsbury refrigerated classic pizza crust

1 unpeeled large Red Delicious apple, thinly sliced

$\frac{1}{2}$ teaspoon sugar

3 cups cubed cooked chicken breast

$\frac{1}{3}$ cup cooked real bacon bits (from 3-oz package)

2 medium green onions, sliced (2 tablespoons)

$1\frac{1}{2}$ cups shredded pepper Jack cheese (6 oz)

$1\frac{1}{2}$ cups shredded Cheddar cheese (6 oz)

Niki Plourde | **Gardner, MA**

Niki Plourde says her husband is "more of a meat and potato kind of guy" who doesn't like chicken, so she didn't expect him to like her recipe. "But he loved it. It's actually the only way he'll eat chicken," she says. She takes pride in going to college later in life, where she is majoring in liberal arts. "It's not easy and I'm darn proud of myself for finally doing it." She traveled the country with her husband in an 18-wheeler for a year and a half. "We had a microwave, an electric skillet and a portable stove, which works like an oven."

---

category winner

apple-jack chicken pizza with caramelized onions

8 servings | Prep Time: **40 minutes** | Start to Finish: **1 hour**

1 In 12-inch skillet, melt 2 tablespoons of the butter over medium heat. Add sweet onions and thyme; cook about 20 minutes, stirring occasionally, until soft and golden. Stir in salt and pepper. Remove onions from skillet; set aside.

2 Heat oven to 425°F. Spray large cookie sheet with cooking spray. Unroll pizza crust dough on cookie sheet; press dough into 14×10-inch rectangle. Bake 7 to 11 minutes or until light golden brown. Reduce oven temperature to 375°F.

3 Meanwhile, in same skillet, melt remaining 1 tablespoon butter over medium heat. Add apple and sugar; cook 4 to 6 minutes, stirring occasionally, until sugar is melted and apple is slightly soft.

4 Spread onion mixture over partially baked crust. Top evenly with chicken, apple mixture, bacon, green onions and cheeses.

5 Bake 10 to 20 minutes longer or until cheeses are melted and crust is golden brown.

High Altitude (3500–6500 ft): No change.

1 Serving: Calories 450; Total Fat 21g (Saturated Fat 12g; Trans Fat 1g); Cholesterol 100mg; Sodium 890mg; Total Carbohydrate 32g (Dietary Fiber 1g) Exchanges: $1\frac{1}{2}$ Starch, $\frac{1}{2}$ Other Carbohydrate, 1 Vegetable, $3\frac{1}{2}$ Lean Meat, 2 Fat Carbohydrate Choices: 2

1 can (13.8 oz) Pillsbury refrigerated classic pizza crust

¼ cup whiskey-flavored or regular barbecue sauce

1 tablespoon grape jelly

¼ teaspoon pepper

¼ cup chopped sweet onion (such as Maui or Walla Walla)

1½ cups cubed cooked chicken breast

⅓ cup cashew pieces

2 tablespoons chopped fresh cilantro

1 cup finely shredded mozzarella and Parmesan cheese blend or Italian cheese blend (4 oz)

¾ cup French-fried onions (from 2.8-oz can)

8 fresh cilantro sprigs, if desired

Debbie Finley | Austin, TX

As a busy grad school student, **Debbie Finley**'s specialty for the moment is "one-pot meals with easy clean up." She loves adapting recipes and enjoys shopping for authentic Indian, Italian, Mexican and Spanish spices to make her recipes more authentic and interesting. This pizza recipe combines flavors from some of her husband's favorite foods, including Chinese cashew chicken, barbecue chicken and those "addictive French-fried onions in a can." It has "a unique cornucopia of textures and popular flavors," she says.

barbecue cashew-chicken pizza with french-fried onions

8 servings | Prep Time: **20 minutes** | Start to Finish: **40 minutes**

1 Heat oven to 400°F. Spray 13×9-inch pan or 12-inch pizza pan with cooking spray. Unroll pizza crust dough on pan; press dough to edges of pan. Bake 8 to 12 minutes or until golden brown.

2 Meanwhile, in medium bowl, mix barbecue sauce, jelly, pepper and chopped onion. Spread evenly over partially baked crust. Top with chicken, cashews, chopped cilantro and cheese.

3 Bake 8 to 13 minutes longer or until cheese is melted and crust is deep golden brown.

4 Sprinkle French-fried onions over pizza. Bake 2 to 3 minutes longer or until onions are golden. Garnish with cilantro sprigs.

High Altitude (3500–6500 ft): In step 1, bake 10 to 14 minutes.

1 Serving: Calories 300; Total Fat 11g (Saturated Fat 4g; Trans Fat 1g); Cholesterol 35mg; Sodium 600mg; Total Carbohydrate 33g (Dietary Fiber 0g) **Exchanges:** 1 Starch, 1 Other Carbohydrate, 2 Very Lean Meat, 2 Fat **Carbohydrate Choices:** 2

2 teaspoons olive oil

1 teaspoon cornmeal

1 can (13.8 oz) Pillsbury refrigerated classic pizza crust

1/2 cup refrigerated Alfredo sauce (from 10-oz container)

1 cup shredded Italian cheese blend (4 oz)

1/4 cup crumbled Gorgonzola cheese (1 oz)

1 package (6 oz) refrigerated roasted chicken breast strips, chopped

3/4 cup sliced fresh mushrooms

1/2 cup sliced red onion

1/2 cup chopped walnuts

1 clove garlic, finely chopped

1/4 cup lightly packed fresh basil leaves, thinly sliced

chicken alfredo gorgonzola-walnut pizza

6 servings | Prep Time: **20 minutes** | Start to Finish: **40 minutes**

1 Heat oven to 375°F. Brush large cookie sheet with 1 teaspoon of the oil; sprinkle evenly with cornmeal. Unroll pizza crust dough on cookie sheet; press dough into 14×12-inch rectangle. Brush dough with remaining 1 teaspoon oil. Bake 10 to 14 minutes or until light golden brown.

2 Spread Alfredo sauce evenly over partially baked crust. Sprinkle with cheeses, chicken, mushrooms, onion, walnuts and garlic.

3 Bake 10 to 18 minutes longer or until crust is golden brown. Sprinkle with basil.

High Altitude (3500–6500 ft): No change.

1 **Serving:** Calories 450; Total Fat 24g (Saturated Fat 10g; Trans Fat 0g); Cholesterol 60mg; Sodium 920mg; Total Carbohydrate 36g (Dietary Fiber 1g) **Exchanges:** 1 1/2 Starch, 1 Other Carbohydrate, 2 1/2 Medium-Fat Meat, 2 Fat **Carbohydrate Choices:** 2 1/2

Kathy Sepich | **Gresham, OR**

Kathy Sepich loves to experiment in the kitchen, "tossing" together whatever is available. She says, "I've played in the kitchen since I was old enough to stir something in a bowl." Kathy's house reflects her passion for antiques. "I love to create ways to display or decorate with something that is no longer useful in its original form." An old porcelain radiator on her kitchen counter displays bottles of oils and vinegars. Kathy's favorite family meal is rosemary pork roast, garlic mashed potatoes and green beans with bacon.

1 can (13.8 oz) Pillsbury refrigerated classic pizza crust
5 all-beef hot dogs
1 tablespoon olive oil
1 clove garlic, finely chopped
1 cup chili with beans (from 15-oz can)
1 medium onion, chopped (1/2 cup)
1/2 cup chopped dill pickles
1 cup shredded mild Cheddar cheese (4 oz)
1 to 2 tablespoons ketchup
1 to 2 tablespoons yellow mustard

chili-cheese dog pizza

6 servings | Prep Time: **20 minutes** | Start to Finish: **45 minutes**

1   Heat oven to 400°F. Spray large cookie sheet with cooking spray. Unroll pizza crust dough on cookie sheet; press dough into 13×9-inch rectangle. Pinch edges of dough to form rim.

2   Generously prick hot dogs with fork to prevent curling; cut diagonally into 1/4-inch slices (about 9 to 10 slices per hot dog). Place slices on dough; press down gently. Mix oil and garlic; drizzle over dough and hot dogs.

3   Bake 15 to 18 minutes or until crust is golden brown. Meanwhile, in 1-quart saucepan, heat chili over medium-low heat 4 to 5 minutes, stirring occasionally, until hot.

4   Spoon chili randomly over hot dog slices; spread evenly to cover. Sprinkle with onion, pickles and cheese.

5   Bake 2 to 3 minutes longer or until cheese is melted. Drizzle ketchup and mustard in diagonal pattern over pizza.

High Altitude (3500-6500 ft): No change.

1 **Serving:** Calories 430; Total Fat 22g (Saturated Fat 9g; Trans Fat 1g); Cholesterol 40mg; Sodium 1,360mg; Total Carbohydrate 42g (Dietary Fiber 2g) **Exchanges:** 1 1/2 Starch, 1 Other Carbohydrate, 1 1/2 High-Fat Meat, 2 Fat Carbohydrate **Choices:** 3

Robin Hyde | **Deland, FL**

She may be "just an ordinary American" cooking in "just an ordinary kitchen," but **Robin Hyde** hit it out of the ballpark with this sporty pizza. With hot dogs, chili, onions and more, it combines the flavors of an American sporting event on top of a pizza. Robin was having "a rough day at the office" when she learned she was a finalist and says, "It really boosted my spirits!" Robin and her husband traveled to Romania a few years ago, and they also taught English in Bulgaria for six months.

2 tablespoons butter or margarine

2 cloves garlic, finely chopped

1 box (9 oz) frozen spinach, thawed, squeezed to drain

1 can (13.8 oz) Pillsbury refrigerated classic pizza crust

8 oz uncooked ground turkey breast

1/4 teaspoon salt

1/4 teaspoon freshly ground pepper

1/4 cup mango chutney

1/4 cup blanched slivered almonds

1 cup crumbled Gorgonzola cheese (4 oz)

2 green onions, thinly sliced (2 tablespoons)

Amy Brnger | Portsmouth, NH

Amy Brnger's last name is Czech, and because it has only one vowel, people commonly assume she's misspelled her name. She likes the sweet/savory/crunchy/chewy combination of this pizza, and says it's a nice change from the typical tomato and cheese variety. Amy and her husband spent a year in Japan, where they learned a lot about Japanese pottery and food. Now she likes to use tofu, seitan and other Asian ingredients in her cooking. Her favorite ingredient, in fact, is sesame oil, which she says enlivens any vegetable or starch.

chutney pizza with turkey, spinach and gorgonzola

6 servings | Prep Time: **25 minutes** | Start to Finish: **40 minutes**

1 Heat oven to 425°F. Spray 13×9-inch pan with cooking spray.

2 In 10-inch nonstick skillet, melt 1 tablespoon of the butter over low heat. Add garlic; cook, stirring occasionally, until tender. Add spinach. Increase heat to medium; cook 2 to 3 minutes, stirring occasionally, until liquid from the spinach has evaporated and mixture is thoroughly heated. Remove spinach mixture to a bowl.

3 Unroll pizza crust dough in pan; press dough to edges of pan. Bake 7 to 10 minutes or until light golden brown.

4 Meanwhile, add remaining 1 tablespoon butter to skillet; melt over medium heat. Add turkey; cook 4 to 6 minutes, stirring frequently, until no longer pink; drain. Stir in salt and pepper; remove from heat.

5 Cut up large fruit pieces in chutney if necessary. Spread chutney evenly over partially baked crust. Top chutney evenly with turkey and spinach mixture. Sprinkle with almonds and cheese.

6 Bake 10 to 12 minutes longer or until cheese is melted and crust is golden brown. Immediately sprinkle with onions. To serve, cut with serrated knife.

High Altitude (3500-6500 ft): No change.

1 Serving: Calories 370; Total Fat 16g (Saturated Fat 7g; Trans Fat 0g); Cholesterol 50mg; Sodium 890mg; Total Carbohydrate 38g (Dietary Fiber 2g) **Exchanges:** 2 Starch, 1/2 Other Carbohydrate, 2 Very Lean Meat, 2 1/2 Fat **Carbohydrate Choices:** 2 1/2

1 can (13.8 oz) Pillsbury refrigerated classic pizza crust

2 tablespoons olive oil

1/2 lb uncooked chicken breast tenders (not breaded)

2 tablespoons butter or margarine

1 1/2 cups thinly sliced onions

1 package (8 oz) sliced fresh portobello mushrooms

3 cloves garlic, finely chopped

3/4 cup sweet Marsala wine or chicken broth

1/2 cup whipping cream

2 tablespoons chopped fresh Italian (flat-leaf) parsley

1/4 teaspoon salt, if desired

1/4 teaspoon pepper

1 1/2 cups shredded mozzarella cheese (6 oz)

1/2 cup shredded Parmesan cheese

Sherrie Reid | **Jenks, OK**

"Brutally honest" is how **Sherrie Reid** describes her family's feedback on her recipe ideas. So when they told her that her pizza was wonderful, she felt good. "Once I completed the recipe and sent it in, I decided not to make it again for good luck," says Sherrie. When she learned she was a finalist, she tried to act normal but froze. "I wanted to scream but I was in the bank lobby," she says. "I got to my car, called my sister and we both screamed into the phone."

creamy chicken marsala pizza

8 servings | Prep Time: **50 minutes** | Start to Finish: **1 hour 5 minutes**

1 Heat oven to 400°F. Spray 13×9-inch pan with cooking spray. Unroll pizza crust dough in pan; press dough to edges of pan. Bake 11 to 14 minutes or until golden brown.

2 Meanwhile, in 10-inch skillet, heat 1 tablespoon of the oil over medium-high heat. Add chicken; cook about 7 minutes, turning frequently, until lightly browned. Remove chicken from skillet; cut into 1/4-inch pieces. Set aside.

3 To same skillet, add remaining 1 tablespoon oil and the butter. Add onions and mushrooms; cook over medium-high heat about 7 minutes, stirring frequently, until tender. Stir in garlic; cook 1 minute longer. Stir in wine; cook 4 to 5 minutes, stirring occasionally, until wine is reduced by half (about 6 tablespoons). Stir in whipping cream, parsley, salt, pepper and chicken. Reduce heat; simmer uncovered about 5 minutes, stirring occasionally, until mixture is thick and creamy.

4 Sprinkle pizza crust with 3/4 cup of the mozzarella cheese and 1/4 cup of the Parmesan cheese. Spoon chicken mixture evenly over cheeses. Top with remaining cheeses. Bake 10 to 12 minutes longer or until cheeses are melted and crust is golden brown.

High Altitude (3500–6500 ft): No change.

1 Serving: Calories 370; Total Fat 19g (Saturated Fat 9g; Trans Fat 0g); Cholesterol 55mg; Sodium 640mg; Total Carbohydrate 29g (Dietary Fiber 0g) **Exchanges:** 1 Starch, 1 Other Carbohydrate, 2 Very Lean Meat, 3 1/2 Fat **Carbohydrate Choices:** 2

1 can (13.8 oz) Pillsbury refrigerated classic pizza crust
¼ cup olive oil
½ teaspoon black peppercorns
¼ teaspoon crushed red pepper flakes
2 dried bay leaves
1 box (9 oz) frozen spinach
½ cup ricotta cheese
1 container (5.2 oz) garlic-and-herbs spreadable cheese
¾ cup shredded mozzarella cheese
¾ cup shredded Swiss or Emmentaler cheese

Sherry Johnston |
Green Cove Springs, FL

Sherry Johnston's kitchen floats. That's because she lives on a 40-foot boat. Baking while sailing can present challenges, says Sherry. Take the case of a cake: "Even with an oven that swings with the motion of the boat, it can be still quite a trick keeping the batter within the confines of the pan and the ingredients on the counter," she says. Years ago, Sherry ordered a spinach pizza at a pizza restaurant. It was "love at first bite." Sherry's recipe successfully re-creates the great taste, she says.

florentine pizza with seasoned oil

6 servings | Prep Time: **20 minutes** | Start to Finish: **40 minutes**

1 Heat oven to 400°F. Spray large cookie sheet with cooking spray, or line with cooking parchment paper. Unroll pizza crust dough on cookie sheet; press dough into 13-inch round. Bake 8 to 12 minutes or until lightly browned.

2 Meanwhile, in 8-inch nonstick skillet, mix oil, black peppercorns, red pepper flakes and bay leaves. Cook over medium heat 3 to 5 minutes, stirring occasionally, until bay leaves start to brown. Remove from heat; set aside.

3 Cook spinach in microwave as directed on box. Drain spinach; cool 5 minutes. Carefully squeeze with paper towels to drain.

4 In small bowl, mix ricotta cheese and spreadable cheese until well blended. Spread evenly over partially baked crust. Top with spinach, mozzarella cheese and Swiss cheese.

5 Bake 12 to 17 minutes longer or until cheeses are melted and crust is deep golden brown.

6 Pour oil mixture through fine-mesh strainer into jar or small pitcher; discard seasonings. Drizzle each serving with oil.

High Altitude (3500–6500 ft): No change.

1 Serving: Calories 460; Total Fat 28g (Saturated Fat 12g; Trans Fat 0g); Cholesterol 50mg; Sodium 700mg; Total Carbohydrate 36g (Dietary Fiber 1g) **Exchanges:** 1½ Starch, 1 Other Carbohydrate, 2 High-Fat Meat, 2 Fat **Carbohydrate Choices:** 2½

1 can (13.8 oz) Pillsbury refrigerated classic pizza crust

⅓ cup apricot preserves

8 oz uncooked bratwurst links (original flavor), casings removed

1 large onion, chopped (1 cup)

1 cup well-drained sauerkraut (from 14-oz can)

1½ cups shredded Monterey Jack cheese (6 oz)

german-style sausage pizza

6 servings | Prep Time: **20 minutes** | Start to Finish: **40 minutes**

1 Heat oven to 400°F. Spray 12-inch pizza pan with cooking spray. Unroll pizza crust dough on pan; press dough to edge of pan. Bake 8 to 12 minutes or until light golden brown. Brush preserves over dough; set aside.

2 Spray 10-inch skillet with cooking spray. Add sausage, onion and sauerkraut; cook over medium-high heat 5 to 7 minutes, stirring occasionally and breaking up sausage, until sausage is no longer pink. Remove sausage mixture with slotted spoon; spoon evenly over preserves on crust. Sprinkle cheese over top.

3 Bake 13 to 19 minutes or until cheese is melted and crust is golden brown.

High Altitude (3500–6500 ft): In step 3, bake 13 to 17 minutes.

1 Serving: Calories 420; Total Fat 19g (Saturated Fat 9g; Trans Fat 0g); Cholesterol 40mg; Sodium 1,150mg; Total Carbohydrate 49g (Dietary Fiber 1g) Exchanges: 1½ Starch, 1½ Other Carbohydrate, 1½ High-Fat Meat, 1½ Fat Carbohydrate Choices: 3

Eva Hukalo | Toledo, OH

Needing a quick supper one night, **Eva Hukalo** rummaged around in her kitchen and whipped up this tangy, savory pizza with the ingredients she had on hand. Her husband told her to type up the recipe before she forgot it. Now she serves it when she's in a hurry and wants a tasty meal. Eva, who is Greek and Italian, remembers making sun-dried tomatoes with her grandmother. She says she "lives in the kitchen" and owns just about every small appliance ever made. Eva was a Bake-Off® Contest finalist once before—nearly 30 years ago.

2 tablespoons olive oil

Cornmeal, if desired

3 oz thickly sliced pancetta, chopped
($^3/_4$ cup)

5 cups chopped iceberg or romaine lettuce

1$^1/_2$ cups ($^1/_2$-inch cubes) skinned rotisserie
chicken breast

$^3/_4$ cup cubed fresh mozzarella cheese

2 plum (Roma) tomatoes, chopped ($^3/_4$ cup)

$^1/_4$ cup sun-dried tomatoes in oil, drained,
chopped

3 tablespoons fresh basil leaves, thinly
sliced

1 can (13.8 oz) Pillsbury refrigerated classic
pizza crust

2 teaspoons Italian seasoning

$^1/_2$ cup shredded Asiago cheese (2 oz)

$^1/_2$ to $^3/_4$ cup red wine vinaigrette dressing

$^1/_4$ cup crumbled sweet or regular Gorgonzola cheese, if desired

Basil sprigs or basil leaves, thinly sliced

Bob Gadsby | Great Falls, MT

Bob Gadsby loves trying new restaurants and duplicating the dishes when he returns home. Bob noticed that chopped salads were becoming popular at restaurants. Instead of simply serving bread on the side, he added a pizza crust underneath. "I made the recipe the first time for a casual get-together," says Bob. "We were entertaining a mix of kids and adults and it was well received by everyone." Pizza and barbecue are Bob's cooking specialties and his favorite holiday food is corn pudding with caramelized onions. "Unbelievably good!" he says.

italian chopped salad pizzas

4 individual pizzas | Prep Time: **40 minutes** | Start to Finish: **55 minutes**

1 Heat oven to 425°F. Lightly brush large cookie sheet with 1 tablespoon of the oil; sprinkle with cornmeal. In 8-inch skillet, cook pancetta over medium-high heat, stirring occasionally, until crisp; drain.

2 In large bowl, mix lettuce, chicken, mozzarella cheese, plum tomatoes, sun-dried tomatoes, sliced basil and pancetta; set aside.

3 Unroll pizza crust dough; cut into 4 rectangles, using pizza cutter. Place rectangles on cookie sheet. Press each rectangle into 8×6-inch oval, folding over edges of dough to form a rim. Brush remaining 1 tablespoon oil over dough ovals; sprinkle evenly with Italian seasoning and Asiago cheese. Bake 11 to 13 minutes or until crusts are golden brown and cheese is melted.

4 Pour dressing over salad mixture; toss to mix. Mound about 2 cups of the salad mixture onto each pizza crust; sprinkle with Gorgonzola cheese. Garnish with basil.

High Altitude (3500–6500 ft): No change.

1 Individual Pizza: Calories 690; Total Fat 35g (Saturated Fat 11g; Trans Fat 0g); Cholesterol 85mg; Sodium 1,810mg; Total Carbohydrate 55g (Dietary Fiber 2g) **Exchanges:** 2 Starch, 1$^1/_2$ Other Carbohydrate, 1 Vegetable, 4 Lean Meat, 4$^1/_2$ Fat **Carbohydrate Choices:** 3$^1/_2$

1 can (13.8 oz) Pillsbury refrigerated classic
    pizza crust
1 medium white potato
1 tablespoon olive oil
1/4 teaspoon salt
1/4 teaspoon pepper
1 box (10 oz) frozen broccoli and cheese
    sauce
2/3 cup sour cream
1 tablespoon ranch dressing
1 cup shredded Colby-Monterey Jack
    cheese blend (4 oz)
5 slices cooked bacon, coarsely chopped
1 small tomato, seeded, chopped (1/2 cup)
2 medium green onions, chopped
    (2 tablespoons)

loaded baked potato pizza

6 servings | Prep Time: **35 minutes** | Start to Finish: **1 hour**

1 Heat oven to 375°F. Spray large cookie sheet with cooking spray.
Unroll pizza crust dough on cookie sheet; press dough into 13×9-
inch rectangle. Bake 10 to 13 minutes or until crust is light golden
brown. Remove from oven; set aside.

2 Meanwhile, pierce potato with fork; place on microwavable paper
towel in microwave oven. Microwave 4 to 5 minutes, turning once,
until tender. Cover; let stand 5 minutes. When potato is cool
enough to handle, peel potato and cut into 1/4-inch cubes (1 cup).
In small bowl, mix potato, oil, salt and pepper; set aside.

3 Cook broccoli in microwave as directed on box. Empty from pouch
into another small bowl to cool slightly; set aside.

4 In another small bowl, mix sour cream and ranch dressing. Spread
mixture over pizza crust to within 1/2 inch of edges of crust.
Sprinkle 1/2 cup of the cheese evenly over sour cream mixture.
Sprinkle with bacon.

5 Spread broccoli mixture and potato mixture evenly over bacon.
Sprinkle tomato, onions and remaining 1/2 cup cheese evenly over
potato mixture.

6 Bake 15 to 22 minutes longer or until crust is golden brown and
cheese is melted. Let stand 5 minutes before cutting.

High Altitude (3500–6500 ft): No change.

1 Serving: Calories 410; Total Fat 20g (Saturated Fat 9g; Trans Fat 0g); Cholesterol 45mg; Sodium 1,060mg; Total
Carbohydrate 42g (Dietary Fiber 2g) **Exchanges:** 2 Starch, 1 Other Carbohydrate, 1 High-Fat Meat, 2 Fat
Carbohydrate Choices: 3

Tracy C. Martinez | **Cheyenne, WY**

Pizza rates as one of
Tracy C. Martinez's all-
time favorite foods. She's
also fond of big baked
potatoes piled with
sour cream, cheese and
bacon. She put her pizza and potato
passions together in her recipe. She
also can whip up a "pretty mean Mexican meal" of enchiladas made from
homemade flour tortillas with pork,
green chili and fideo (a type of noodle).
She learned how to make tortillas
from her grandmother, whose cooking
advice she still follows: "The more you
practice, the better they turn out."

1 can (13.8 oz) Pillsbury refrigerated classic pizza crust

¼ cup butter or margarine

1 large onion, thinly sliced

1 container (5.2 oz) garlic-and-herbs spreadable cheese

¼ cup sliced sun-dried tomatoes in oil, well drained

2 jars (6.5 oz each) marinated artichoke hearts, well drained, coarsely chopped

2 tablespoons finely chopped fresh parsley

3 tablespoons grated Parmesan cheese

luscious artichoke heart pizza

8 servings | Prep Time: **20 minutes** | Start to Finish: **40 minutes**

1 Heat oven to 400°F. Spray 12-inch pizza pan or 13×9-inch pan with cooking spray. Unroll pizza crust dough on pan; press dough to edge of pan. Bake 10 to 12 minutes or until light golden brown.

2 Meanwhile, in 10-inch skillet, cook butter and onion over medium heat 10 to 15 minutes, stirring occasionally, until onion is deep golden brown. Remove from heat; set aside.

3 Spread spreadable cheese evenly over partially baked crust. Spread onion evenly over cheese; top with tomatoes and artichoke hearts.

4 Bake 6 to 11 minutes longer or until crust is golden brown. Sprinkle with parsley and Parmesan cheese. Bake 3 minutes longer. Let stand 5 minutes before cutting.

High Altitude (3500–6500 ft): No change.

1 Serving: Calories 300; Total Fat 16g (Saturated Fat 9g; Trans Fat 0g); Cholesterol 35mg; Sodium 610mg; Total Carbohydrate 30g (Dietary Fiber 2g) **Exchanges:** 1½ Starch, ½ Other Carbohydrate, ½ High-Fat Meat, 2 Fat **Carbohydrate Choices:** 2

Kathryn Morrison | Danville, CA

Kathryn Morrison was in the dentist's chair when she got the call informing her that she was a finalist. The whole dentist's office shared her happiness, she says. "It was a very surreal day!" The idea for her recipe came to her while she was contemplating artichokes and thinking about pizza for dinner. Neighbors declared her new dish "luscious." Kathryn concurs. "It tastes indulgent, looks pretty and is flat-out delicious." She's long felt "a wonderful power in making people happy through food."

1½ tablespoons cornmeal

1 can (13.8 oz) Pillsbury refrigerated classic pizza crust

7 pieces (1 oz each) mozzarella string cheese (from 12-oz package), unwrapped

¼ cup tomato sauce with basil, garlic and oregano or regular tomato sauce (from 8-oz can)

¼ cup chopped fresh basil leaves

½ lb bulk spicy pork sausage

⅓ cup chopped sun-dried tomatoes in oil, drained

1 box (9 oz) frozen spinach, thawed, squeezed to drain

¼ cup sliced ripe olives

¼ cup sliced pimiento-stuffed olives

½ cup crumbled feta cheese (2 oz)

2 cups shredded mozzarella cheese (8 oz)

2 tablespoons olive oil

½ teaspoon Italian seasoning

½ to 1 teaspoon garlic salt

Barbara Williams | **Lawrenceville, GA**

Barbara Williams
wanted to cook a pizza with the ingredients and flavors that she and her husband love. Barbara kept experimenting until she got the right combination. Wonderful flavors burst in your mouth on the first bite and every bite, she says. Barbara grew up in Louisiana ("Cajun food is in my blood") and now lives in Georgia where "our backyard looks like Florida." Thanks to her husband's passion for landscaping, the backyard boasts 50 banana trees and a 15-foot palm tree.

mediterranean pizza with cheese-stuffed crust

8 servings | Prep Time: **25 minutes** | Start to Finish: **45 minutes**

1 Heat oven to 425°F. Spray 12-inch pizza pan with cooking spray. Sprinkle cornmeal evenly over pan. Unroll pizza crust dough on pan; press dough to at least 1 inch beyond edge of pan. Place string cheese on dough along inside edge of crust. Fold edge of dough over cheese, pressing dough down firmly and covering cheese. Pinch dough to seal.

2 Spread tomato sauce evenly over dough. Sprinkle with basil.

3 Heat 10-inch nonstick skillet over medium-high heat. Add sausage; cook 5 to 7 minutes, stirring frequently, until no longer pink; drain. Reduce heat to medium. Stir tomatoes and spinach into sausage until well mixed. Cook 3 to 4 minutes, stirring frequently, until spinach is heated.

4 Spoon sausage mixture evenly over basil on crust. Top with ripe and pimiento-stuffed olives. Sprinkle with feta and mozzarella cheeses.

5 Brush oil on edge of crust; sprinkle Italian seasoning and garlic salt on edge of crust.

6 Bake 15 to 18 minutes or until cheese is melted and crust is deep golden brown. Let stand 2 minutes before cutting.

High Altitude (3500–6500 ft): No change.

1 Serving: Calories 420; Total Fat 23g (Saturated Fat 10g; Trans Fat 0g); Cholesterol 45mg; Sodium 1,060mg; Total Carbohydrate 30g (Dietary Fiber 1g) **Exchanges:** 1 Starch, 1 Other Carbohydrate, 3 Medium-Fat Meat, 1 Fat **Carbohydrate Choices:** 2

1 can (13.8 oz) Pillsbury refrigerated classic pizza crust

4 cups chopped fresh spinach

1/3 cup blanched slivered almonds

2 tablespoons olive oil

2 cups coarsely chopped cooked chicken breast (6 oz)

1/4 cup orange marmalade

3 tablespoons chopped pitted dates (6 dates)

1/2 teaspoon ground fennel or 1/2 teaspoon fennel seed, ground

1/2 teaspoon ground cardamom

1/2 cup crumbled chèvre (goat) cheese (2 oz)

north african–style chicken pizza

8 servings | Prep Time: **20 minutes** | Start to Finish: **35 minutes**

1 Heat oven to 400°F. Unroll pizza crust dough on ungreased 12-inch pizza pan; press dough to edge of pan. Pinch edge of dough to make 1/2-inch rim. Bake 7 to 11 minutes or until light golden brown.

2 Meanwhile, in food processor bowl with metal blade or in blender, place spinach, almonds and oil. Cover; process until smooth. Spread spinach mixture evenly over partially baked crust.

3 In medium bowl, stir chicken, marmalade, dates, fennel and cardamom until well mixed. Spoon chicken mixture evenly over spinach mixture. Sprinkle with cheese.

4 Bake 7 to 11 minutes longer or until crust is golden brown.

High Altitude (3500–6500 ft): No change.

1 Serving: Calories 310; Total Fat 11g (Saturated Fat 3g; Trans Fat 0g); Cholesterol 35mg; Sodium 430mg; Total Carbohydrate 35g (Dietary Fiber 1g) Exchanges: 1 Starch, 1 1/2 Other Carbohydrate, 2 Lean Meat, 1 Fat Carbohydrate Choices: 2

Harrison Carpenter | Longmont, CO

Harrison Carpenter enjoys life with an extra dash of adventure. One of his most memorable cooking challenges was a backpacking trek that greatly limited the ingredients, cooking utensils and equipment available. He also likes to test his endurance on a bike, and logs an average of 150 miles a week, riding "as fast as possible"—a pursuit that once resulted in a near-fatal bike crash. Harrison has gone on to cook many delicious meals, including this exotic and spicy pizza, adapted from a chicken tagine dish he enjoyed at an African restaurant.

12 oz uncooked bacon (about 15 slices), cut into ¹/₂-inch pieces

12 oz uncooked chorizo sausage links, casings removed

1 can (13.8 oz) Pillsbury refrigerated classic pizza crust

¹/₄ cup orange marmalade

2 tablespoons olive oil

3 tablespoons chopped fresh parsley

1 cup dates, coarsely chopped

1¹/₂ cups shredded Monterey Jack cheese (6 oz)

1 large poblano or Anaheim chile, seeded, coarsely chopped (²/₃ cup)

Monika Johnson | **Chicago, IL**

Monika Johnson traces her recipe inspiration to the flavors she enjoyed at a tapas restaurant: sweet date wrapped in savory bacon. Restaurant dishes often spur recipe ideas for Monika, who likes to "draw inspiration from memorable ingredients to create my own 'signature' dishes." She enjoys putting time and thought into her cooking. "Strategizing is the exciting part and cooking is the relaxing part," says Monika. But don't try to lend a hand. "I don't like help in the kitchen. I like to do it all myself—my way."

orange marmalade–chorizo pizza

8 servings | Prep Time: **40 minutes** | Start to Finish: **55 minutes**

1 Heat oven to 425°F. Spray 12-inch pizza pan with cooking spray.

2 In 12-inch nonstick skillet, cook bacon over medium heat 10 to 12 minutes, stirring occasionally, until crisp. Remove bacon with slotted spoon; drain on paper towels. Drain bacon drippings from skillet.

3 In same skillet, cook sausage over medium-high heat 10 to 12 minutes, stirring occasionally and breaking up sausage with spoon, until no longer pink. Remove sausage with slotted spoon; drain well on paper towels.

4 Meanwhile, unroll pizza crust dough on pan; press dough to edge of pan. In small bowl, mix marmalade, oil and parsley; spread evenly over dough. Bake 8 to 9 minutes or until crust is golden brown.

5 Sprinkle partially baked crust evenly with sausage, bacon and dates. Sprinkle with cheese. Sprinkle chile over cheese; press gently into cheese.

6 Bake 7 to 12 minutes longer or until crust is deep golden brown.

High Altitude (3500–6500 ft): In step 4, bake crust 10 to 11 minutes.

1 Serving: Calories 590; Total Fat 33g (Saturated Fat 13g; Trans Fat 0g); Cholesterol 70mg; Sodium 1,270mg; Total Carbohydrate 49g (Dietary Fiber 2g) **Exchanges:** 1 Starch, 2 Other Carbohydrate, 3 High-Fat Meat, 2 Fat **Carbohydrate Choices:** 3

1 can (13.8 oz) Pillsbury refrigerated classic pizza crust

¼ cup red raspberry preserves

¼ cup hickory smoke–flavored barbecue sauce (or other favorite flavor)

2 teaspoons chopped chipotle chiles in adobo sauce (from 7-oz can)

1 package (6 oz) refrigerated grilled chicken breast strips, cubed

½ medium red onion, cut into thin strips

1½ cups shredded mozzarella cheese (6 oz)

¼ cup grated Parmesan cheese

¼ cup chopped fresh cilantro

raspberry-chipotle barbecue chicken pizza

6 servings | Prep Time: **15 minutes** | Start to Finish: **35 minutes**

1 Heat oven to 425°F. Lightly spray 13×9-inch pan with cooking spray. Unroll pizza crust dough in pan; press dough to edges of pan.

2 In small bowl, mix preserves, barbecue sauce and chiles. Spread mixture evenly over dough to within ¼ inch of edges. Top with chicken, onion and cheeses.

3 Bake 12 to 20 minutes or until cheeses are melted and edges are deep golden brown. Sprinkle with cilantro.

High Altitude (3500–6500 ft): No change.

1 Serving: Calories 370; Total Fat 10g (Saturated Fat 5g; Trans Fat 0g); Cholesterol 45mg; Sodium 840mg; Total Carbohydrate 47g (Dietary Fiber 0g) Exchanges: 2 Starch, 1 Other Carbohydrate, 2½ Lean Meat Carbohydrate Choices: 3

Patricia Kalb | Albuquerque, NM

Patricia Kalb likes spicy food and decided to try adding raspberry preserves and chipotle peppers to the sauce for barbecue chicken pizza. Her family loved it, she says. The combination of the flavors is very tasty and appealing, she says, and the heat of the chipotle peppers gives it a little "kick." Patricia and her husband received a European trip as a wedding present and enjoyed "sampling all the delicious food in the various countries."

1 can (13.8 oz) Pillsbury refrigerated classic
   pizza crust
1 lb lean (at least 80%) ground beef
1 medium onion, chopped (1/2 cup)
1/4 cup diced jalapeño chiles*
1/4 teaspoon ground mustard
1/4 teaspoon garlic powder
1 1/2 teaspoons Worcestershire sauce
1 cup chunky-style salsa
1/2 cup grape jelly
2 cups shredded mild Cheddar cheese (8 oz)

southwest sloppy joe pizza

8 servings | Prep Time: **20 minutes** | Start to Finish: **45 minutes**

1 Heat oven to 400°F. Spray large cookie sheet with cooking spray. Unroll pizza crust dough on cookie sheet; press dough into 15×10-inch rectangle. Bake 8 to 10 minutes or until light golden brown.

2 In 10-inch skillet, cook beef, onion and chiles over medium heat 8 to 10 minutes, stirring occasionally, until beef is thoroughly cooked; drain well.

3 Stir mustard, garlic powder, Worcestershire sauce, salsa and jelly into beef mixture. Cook over medium heat 5 to 6 minutes, stirring occasionally, until slightly thickened.

4 Spread beef mixture evenly over partially baked crust. Sprinkle with cheese.

5 Bake 8 to 16 minutes longer or until cheese is melted and crust is golden brown. Let stand 5 minutes before cutting.

*If desired, remove ribs and seeds from chiles before dicing for less heat.

High Altitude (3500–6500 ft): No change.

1 Serving: Calories 400; Total Fat 17g (Saturated Fat 9g; Trans Fat 1g); Cholesterol 65mg; Sodium 800mg; Total Carbohydrate 41g (Dietary Fiber 0g) **Exchanges:** 1 Starch, 1 1/2 Other Carbohydrate, 2 1/2 Medium-Fat Meat, 1 Fat **Carbohydrate Choices:** 3

Chris Batton | North Irwin, PA

Chris Batton had friends coming over to watch a football game, so he decided to make this spicy/sweet pizza, adding jalapeños for an extra kick. The hearty pizza scored big and his wife encouraged him to enter the Bake-Off® Contest. The couple loves to cook, but their 1914-era kitchen was cramped. They solved the problem by eliminating the dining room to create a kitchen big enough for two. "I started cooking at a young age and my father was my biggest teacher," says Chris. He enjoys weekend meals on the grill when it isn't so rushed.

CRUST

1 tablespoon olive oil

2 tablespoons yellow cornmeal

1 can (13.8 oz) Pillsbury refrigerated classic pizza crust

SEASONING BLEND

2 tablespoons grated Asiago cheese

2 tablespoons sesame seed

1 teaspoon garlic powder

1 teaspoon Italian seasoning

1/2 to 1 teaspoon crushed red pepper flakes

TOPPINGS

8 oz fresh mozzarella cheese, cut into 1/4-inch cubes

2 cups shredded mozzarella cheese (8 oz)

1/4 cup chopped dry-pack sun-dried tomatoes

4 oz thinly sliced pancetta or smoked ham, chopped (1/2 cup)

Bee Engelhart | **Bloomfield Hills, MI**

When **Bee Engelhart** was a new bride and novice cook, she was entrusted only with the bread or rolls as her contribution to family potlucks. Since then, both her cooking skills and confidence have "risen" significantly, and now, she says, "If I do bring the bread, it's spectacular!" This pizza was inspired by a flatbread recipe. "It's salty, spicy, creamy, crusty and even a bit sweet," she says. Bee had three goals for 2007: learn to speak Italian, publish her first novel and make it to the Bake-Off® Contest. "Molto bene so far," she says.

---

spicy double-mozzarella pancetta pizza

8 servings | Prep Time: **20 minutes** | Start to Finish: **35 minutes**

1 Heat oven to 425°F. Brush oil on bottom and sides of 15×10-inch pan. Sprinkle cornmeal evenly over bottom of pan. Unroll pizza crust dough in pan; press dough to edges of pan.

2 Bake 6 to 8 minutes or until light golden brown. Meanwhile, in small bowl, mix seasoning blend ingredients.

3 Sprinkle toppings in order listed evenly over partially baked crust. Sprinkle seasoning blend over toppings.

4 Bake 7 to 11 minutes longer or until cheese is melted and crust is golden brown.

High Altitude (3500–6500 ft): No change.

1 Serving: Calories 370; Total Fat 18g (Saturated Fat 9g; Trans Fat 0g); Cholesterol 40mg; Sodium 890mg; Total Carbohydrate 29g (Dietary Fiber 0g) **Exchanges:** 1 1/2 Starch, 1/2 Other Carbohydrate, 2 1/2 Medium-Fat Meat, 1 Fat **Carbohydrate Choices:** 2

1 can (13.8 oz) Pillsbury refrigerated classic pizza crust
8 slices uncooked bacon
¼ cup mayonnaise or salad dressing
¼ cup apricot preserves
6 oz thinly sliced roast turkey breast (from deli)
4 to 5 oz Brie cheese, cut into 4 slices
Parsley sprigs, if desired

turkey, bacon and brie panini with apricot aioli

4 sandwiches | Prep Time: **30 minutes** | Start to Finish: **30 minutes**

1 Heat oven to 375°F. Spray 15×10-inch pan with cooking spray. Unroll pizza crust dough in pan; press dough to edges of pan. Bake 7 to 12 minutes or until light golden brown. Cool 5 minutes.

2 Meanwhile, in 10-inch skillet, cook bacon over medium heat, turning once, until crisp. Remove bacon from skillet; drain on paper towels.

3 In small bowl, make apricot aioli by stirring mayonnaise and preserves until well mixed. Set aside.

4 Cut pizza crust in half crosswise to make 2 rectangles. Remove rectangles from pan; spread half of the apricot aioli evenly over each rectangle. Top 1 rectangle evenly with turkey, bacon and cheese. Add other rectangle, aioli side down. Cut large sandwich in half crosswise; cut each in half diagonally to make 4 sandwiches.

5 Heat 12-inch skillet over medium heat until hot. Place 2 sandwiches in skillet. Place smaller skillet or saucepan on sandwiches to flatten slightly; keep skillet on sandwiches while cooking. Cook 1 to 4 minutes on each side or until cheese is melted and bread is golden brown. Remove from skillet; cover with foil to keep warm. Repeat with remaining 2 sandwiches. Garnish with parsley sprigs.

High Altitude (3500–6500 ft): No change.

1 Sandwich: Calories 630; Total Fat 29g (Saturated Fat 10g; Trans Fat 0g); Cholesterol 90mg; Sodium 1,360mg; Total Carbohydrate 61g (Dietary Fiber 0g) **Exchanges:** 2½ Starch, 1½ Other Carbohydrate, 3½ High-Fat Meat **Carbohydrate Choices:** 4

Kim Frantz | Denver, CO

If you can make a grilled cheese sandwich, says **Kim Frantz**, you can make her panini recipe. Using pizza dough adds a creative edge, she says, and gives it the gourmet appeal of a bistro entrée. Eating at great restaurants and browsing through her collection of Junior League cookbooks provide inspiration for her new recipe creations. Kim was a kindergarten and first-grade teacher for many years, and she encourages parents to make their kitchen a fun place. "Try to involve your kids in the cooking process," she says.

Grand Prize Winner **Carolyn Gurtz,** Gaithersburg, Maryland, was the winner of this category. She received $1 million and a set of kitchen appliances for Double-Delight Peanut Butter Cookies (p. 186). Her cookies combine two classic cookies—a snickerdoodle and a peanut butter—into one.

chapter five

sweet treats

Whether it's a special occasion or an any-time celebration, family and friends will love these quick and easy treats, including cookies, pies, tortes, brownies and bars.

Trends in Sweet Treats Category

Favorite coffee drinks were reflected in many recipes, including mochas, lattes and espresso. Teas, such as green and red teas, also were common ingredients. Dry chai tea mix flavored cookies, scones and biscotti.

Latin was a common ethnic influence. There were many recipes for dulce de leche, tres leches cakes and flans. Several desserts used tortillas as a base or Mojito flavors, such as lime or rum. And brownies were given extra spice by adding cayenne pepper, chipotle chiles or ancho chiles.

Root beer was a popular flavor, with many recipes using root beer extract or crushed root beer barrels. Aromatic lavender chocolates and sugars also were used.

A variety of baking chips were used, such as mint, cappuccino, chocolate-orange, chocolate-cherry, cinnamon, chocolate, vanilla, peanut butter and dark chocolate.

Jams were used in many interesting ways: sweeteners in fruit pies; layers in bars or cakes; mixed into brownies; or drizzled on tarts or slices of pie or cake.

1 cup blanched slivered almonds

2 cups Pillsbury BEST all-purpose unbleached flour

¹/₂ cup sugar

1 cup butter or margarine, cut up

1 cup apricot preserves

¹/₃ cup caramel topping

³/₄ cup unsweetened or sweetened shredded coconut

apricot-caramel-coconut bars

36 bars | Prep Time: **10 minutes** | Start to Finish: **3 hours**

1 Heat oven to 350°F. In food processor bowl with metal blade, place almonds. Cover; process with on-and-off pulses until finely chopped. Add flour, sugar and butter to almonds. Cover; process with on-and-off pulses until mixture looks like coarse crumbs. (Or, finely chop almonds. In large bowl, mix chopped almonds, flour and sugar; cut in butter with pastry blender until mixture looks like coarse crumbs.)

2 In bottom of ungreased 13×9-inch pan, evenly press half of crumb mixture (about 2 ¹/₂ cups).

3 In medium bowl, mix preserves, caramel topping and coconut. Spread evenly over crumb mixture to within ¹/₂ inch of edges. Sprinkle remaining crumb mixture evenly over apricot mixture to edges of pan.

4 Bake 40 to 50 minutes or until edges are golden brown. Cool completely, about 2 hours. For bars, cut into 6 rows by 6 rows.

High Altitude (3500–6500 ft): No change.

1 **Bar:** Calories 140; Total Fat 8g (Saturated Fat 5g; Trans Fat 0g); Cholesterol 15mg; Sodium 50mg; Total Carbohydrate 16g (Dietary Fiber 0g) **Exchanges:** ¹/₂ Starch, ¹/₂ Other Carbohydrate, 1¹/₂ Fat **Carbohydrate Choices:** 1

Linda Hickam | Healdsburg, CA

Linda Hickam's bars are simple and require just a few ingredients. The blended flavors of apricot, caramel and coconut with a hint of almond should appeal to most everyone, she says. Linda gets teased for wanting to stay home some Saturday nights just to bake cookies. Years ago, she developed a chocolate chip cookie recipe "that people still beg me for," she says. Linda explains that chicken with polenta is her favorite family meal because, "I'm very Italian." She has memories of her Italian grandmothers preparing lots of wonderful food.

1 roll (16.5 oz) Pillsbury refrigerated sugar
  cookies
1 package (1.1 oz) chai tea latte mix (from
  8.8-oz box)
½ cup caramel sundae syrup
2 tablespoons Pillsbury BEST all-purpose
  flour
½ cup ground walnuts

caramel chai bars

16 bars | Prep Time: **20 minutes** | Start to Finish: **2 hours 40 minutes**

1 Heat oven to 350°F. In large bowl, knead cookie dough and dry chai mix until well blended.
2 Break up ¾ of the chai dough in ungreased 8-inch square pan. Press dough evenly in bottom of pan. (If dough is sticky, use floured fingers.) Bake 12 to 17 minutes or until light golden brown.
3 Meanwhile, in small bowl, mix caramel syrup and flour. In another small bowl, knead remaining ¼ of chai dough and the walnuts.
4 Gently drizzle caramel mixture evenly over partially baked crust. Crumble walnut chai dough evenly over caramel.
5 Bake 22 to 29 minutes longer or until top is golden brown and firm to the touch and caramel is bubbly. Cool completely, about 1 hour 30 minutes. For bars, cut into 4 rows by 4 rows.

High Altitude (3500–6500 ft): In step 2, bake 15 to 20 minutes. In step 5, bake 29 to 32 minutes.

1 **Bar:** Calories 190; Total Fat 9g (Saturated Fat 2g; Trans Fat 2g); Cholesterol 10mg; Sodium 140mg; Total Carbohydrate 27g (Dietary Fiber 0g) **Exchanges:** ½ Starch, 1½ Other Carbohydrate, 1½ Fat **Carbohydrate Choices:** 2

Kerstin Sinkevicius | Somerville, MA

"I fell in love with chai lattes several years ago and almost immediately thought it would be great to spice sugar cookies with," said **Kerstin Sinkevicius**. The caramel inspiration came from a favorite bar cookie. "I knew the fusing of the two flavors, along with the walnuts, would be really delicious." Kerstin's been on a winning streak. In December 2006 she won a two-seat sports car from a credit card promotion. She is most proud of getting her Ph.D., which took "six long years of hard work," she says.

CRUST

1 Pillsbury refrigerated pie crust (from 15-oz box), softened as directed on box

FILLING

1 package (8 oz) cream cheese, softened

1 cup whole or 2% milk

1 box (4-serving size) vanilla instant pudding and pie filling mix

1/2 cup frozen (thawed) limeade concentrate

1 1/2 teaspoons rum extract

TOPPING

1 1/2 cups whipping cream

1/4 cup powdered sugar

3/4 to 1 1/2 teaspoons mint extract

GARNISHES, IF DESIRED

Fresh mint sprigs

Lime slices

Ayofemi Wright | Atlanta, GA

Pies hold a special place in the cooking life and times of **Ayofemi Wright**. She became interested in cooking as a little girl, watching her dad make lemon meringue pies. Not content to simply observe, she says, "I attempted to bake an apple pie when I was four years old, using only cut-up apples, 'pie dough' (flour moistened with water), and nothing else!" These days her favorite dessert is red velvet cake. Ayofemi says her Bake-Off® recipe was inspired by the fresh flavors of a Mojito cocktail.

---

creamy mojito pie

8 servings | Prep Time: **15 minutes** | Start to Finish: **1 hour 45 minutes**

1 Heat oven to 450°F. Make pie crust as directed on box for One-Crust Baked Shell using 9-inch glass pie plate. Bake 10 to 12 minutes or until light golden brown. Cool completely on cooling rack, about 15 minutes.

2 In large bowl, beat cream cheese with electric mixer on low speed until creamy. Add remaining filling ingredients; beat on low speed about 30 seconds or until blended. Beat on medium speed 2 minutes, scraping bowl occasionally, until thickened and creamy. Spoon filling evenly into pie crust; refrigerate while making topping.

3 In same bowl, beat topping ingredients on medium speed until stiff peaks form. Spread topping evenly over filling. Refrigerate about 1 hour or until set.

4 Garnish pie with mint sprigs and lime slices. Cover and refrigerate any remaining pie.

High Altitude (3500–6500 ft): No change.

1 **Serving:** Calories 480; Total Fat 32g (Saturated Fat 18g; Trans Fat 1g); Cholesterol 90mg; Sodium 400mg; Total Carbohydrate 43g (Dietary Fiber 0g) **Exchanges:** 1 Starch, 2 Other Carbohydrate, 6 Fat **Carbohydrate Choices:** 3

1/4 cup dry-roasted peanuts, finely chopped
1/4 cup granulated sugar
1/2 teaspoon ground cinnamon
1/2 cup creamy peanut butter
1/2 cup powdered sugar
1 roll (16.5 oz) Pillsbury refrigerated peanut butter cookies, well chilled

Carolyn Gurtz | Gaithersburg, MD

Carolyn Gurtz loves baking pies and yeast rolls. Her talents have earned blue ribbons and other awards from her county fair—now on display in her kitchen. She says this peanut butter cookie recipe is perfect for the modern baker because it's so easy to make. "The cookies taste even better than if I spent more time making the dough from scratch," she says. When her son smelled them baking, he came running upstairs to try one. Her passion is baking; yeast rolls are her specialty.

grand prize winner
category winner

double-delight peanut butter cookies

24 cookies | Prep Time: **45 minutes** | Start to Finish: **45 minutes**

1 Heat oven to 375°F. In small bowl, mix chopped peanuts, granulated sugar and cinnamon; set aside.

2 In another small bowl, stir peanut butter and powdered sugar until completely blended. Shape mixture into 24 (1-inch) balls.

3 Cut roll of cookie dough into 12 slices. Cut each slice in half crosswise to make 24 pieces; flatten slightly. Shape 1 cookie dough piece around 1 peanut butter ball, covering completely. Repeat with remaining dough and balls.

4 Roll each covered ball in peanut mixture; gently pat mixture completely onto balls. On ungreased large cookie sheets, place balls 2 inches apart. Spray bottom of drinking glass with cooking spray; press into remaining peanut mixture. Flatten each ball to 1/2-inch thickness with bottom of glass. Sprinkle any remaining peanut mixture evenly on tops of cookies; gently press into dough.

5 Bake 7 to 12 minutes or until edges are golden brown. Cool 1 minute; remove from cookie sheets to cooling rack. Store tightly covered.

High Altitude (3500-6500 ft): No change.

1 Cookie: Calories 150; Total Fat 7g (Saturated Fat 2g; Trans Fat 1g); Cholesterol 0mg; Sodium 125mg; Total Carbohydrate 17g (Dietary Fiber 0g) **Exchanges:** 1 Starch, 1 1/2 Fat **Carbohydrate Choices:** 1

COOKIES

1 box (20 oz) Pillsbury chocolate frosted
  brownie mix
$^1/_2$ cup crunchy peanut butter
2 eggs
1 teaspoon vanilla
$^2/_3$ cup milk chocolate chips

TOPPING

Frosting packet from brownie mix
$^1/_3$ cup crunchy peanut butter
$^1/_4$ cup butter or margarine, softened
2 tablespoons dry-roasted peanuts, finely
  chopped

Stephanie Hollowell | Dallas, TX

Stephanie Hollowell intended her cookies to be like Whoopie Pies, but they wouldn't cooperate. So she said, "Fine! You're now going to be thumbprint cookies." The result: an easy drop cookie that tastes like an indulgent treat. She likes trying to create her friends' "dream desserts" and enjoys the scientific side of baking "because it's one big chemistry experiment." She once spent all night assembling hundreds of individual desserts she made for a friend's wedding. A painter, Stephanie's paintings have won top awards in the Texas State Fair.

fudgy chocolate-peanut butter thumbprints

2 dozen cookies | Prep Time: **1 hour** | Start to Finish: **1 hour**

1 Heat oven to 350°F. Lightly spray large cookie sheets with cooking spray, or line with cooking parchment paper.

2 Reserve frosting packet from brownie mix. In large bowl, beat brownie mix, $^1/_2$ cup peanut butter, the eggs and vanilla with electric mixer on low speed 20 seconds. Beat on high speed 30 to 40 seconds or until completely mixed. Stir in chocolate chips.

3 Drop 24 heaping tablespoons of dough 2 inches apart onto cookie sheets. Press thumb into center of each cookie to make indentation, but do not press all the way to cookie sheet (if dough sticks to thumb, spray thumb with cooking spray). Bake 9 to 11 minutes or until almost no indentation remains when touched. Cool 1 minute; remove from cookie sheets to cooling rack. Cool completely, about 20 minutes.

4 In small bowl, beat contents of reserved frosting packet, $^1/_3$ cup peanut butter and the butter with electric mixer on medium speed until smooth. Fill each thumbprint indentation with 2 teaspoons frosting mixture, spreading slightly; sprinkle with peanuts. Let stand until frosting mixture is set. Store loosely covered in single layer.

High Altitude (3500-6500 ft): No change.

1 **Cookie:** Calories 120; Total Fat 9g (Saturated Fat 3g; Trans Fat 0g); Cholesterol 20mg; Sodium 60mg; Total Carbohydrate 6g (Dietary Fiber 0g) **Exchanges:** $^1/_2$ Other Carbohydrate, $^1/_2$ High-Fat Meat, 1 Fat **Carbohydrate Choices:** $^1/_2$

fudgy peanut butter sandwich cookies

18 cookies | Prep Time: **1 hour 10 minutes** | Start to Finish: **1 hour 55 minutes**

COOKIES

1 roll (16.5 oz) Pillsbury refrigerated peanut butter cookies

1 cup plus 2 tablespoons honey-roasted peanuts, coarsely ground*

PEANUT BUTTER FUDGE FILLING

1/2 cup butter or margarine

1/2 cup creamy peanut butter

2 teaspoons vanilla

2 1/3 cups powdered sugar

GANACHE

1 cup semisweet chocolate chips

2 tablespoons whipping cream

*Grind peanuts in food processor using on-and-off pulses.

1 In large bowl, break up cookie dough. Mix in 1 cup of the peanuts. Cover; refrigerate about 30 minutes or until well chilled.

2 Heat oven to 375°F. Spray cookie sheets with cooking spray, or line with cooking parchment paper. Shape dough into 36 (1 1/4-inch) balls. Place balls 2 inches apart on cookie sheets. Flatten to 1/2-inch thickness with lightly floured drinking glass. Bake 9 to 11 minutes or until edges are golden brown. Cool 5 minutes; remove from cookie sheets to cooling rack. Cool completely, about 30 minutes.

3 Meanwhile, in 2-quart saucepan, melt butter and peanut butter over medium heat, stirring occasionally. Remove from heat; stir in vanilla. Cool 1 minute. Stir in powdered sugar. When cool enough to handle, knead filling several times until powdered sugar is thoroughly blended. Shape into log, about 9 inches long and 2 inches in diameter. Cut into 18 (1/2-inch) slices, reshaping slices into round shape if necessary. Cover with plastic wrap; set aside.

4 When ready to assemble cookies, place 1 filling slice on bottom of 1 cookie; top with another cookie, bottom side down, and press together slightly. Repeat with remaining cookies.

5 In microwavable bowl, microwave chocolate chips and cream uncovered on High about 1 minute, stirring twice, until melted. Spoon heaping 1 teaspoonful on top of each cookie. Sprinkle with remaining ground peanuts. Let stand 10 minutes or until ganache is set. Store tightly covered in single layer at room temperature.

High Altitude (3500–6500 ft): No change.

1 Sandwich Cookie: Calories 380; Total Fat 22g (Saturated Fat 8g; Trans Fat 1g); Cholesterol 20mg; Sodium 190mg; Total Carbohydrate 40g (Dietary Fiber 2g) **Exchanges:** 1/2 Starch, 2 Other Carbohydrate, 1/2 High-Fat Meat, 3 1/2 Fat Carbohydrate Choices: 2 1/2

Beverley Rossell | Morgantown, IN

Beverley Rossell learned to cook by watching her great-aunt prepare food for the hired hands on her 200-acre farm and from her father, a fireman who cooked for his crew. Beverley's entry pairs peanut butter and chocolate: a sandwich cookie with a peanut butter–fudge center, topped with ganache. The recipe is scrumptious and fun to make, she says. Beverley has entered her poetry, essays and jingles in contests, and once won $10,000. She's most proud of her unpublished novel, *Ashes of Roses*.

heavenly caramel pie

1 Pillsbury refrigerated pie crust (from 15-oz box), softened as directed on box

1 1/2 cups caramel topping (from two 12.25-oz jars)

1/4 cup chopped pecans

2 packages (8 oz each) cream cheese, softened

1 container (8 oz) frozen whipped topping, thawed (3 cups)

1/2 cup pecan halves

10 servings | Prep Time: **15 minutes** | Start to Finish: **2 hours 45 minutes**

1 Heat oven to 450°F. Make pie crust as directed on box for One-Crust Baked Shell using 9-inch glass pie plate. Bake 10 to 12 minutes or until light golden brown. Cool completely on cooling rack, about 15 minutes.

2 In small bowl, mix 1/4 cup of the caramel topping and the chopped pecans. Spread mixture evenly over bottom of cooled pie crust.

3 In large bowl, beat cream cheese and 1 cup of the caramel topping with electric mixer on medium speed until well blended. Fold in whipped topping just until blended (do not overmix). Spoon cream cheese mixture into pie crust. Refrigerate at least 2 hours until set.

4 Arrange pecan halves on top of pie; drizzle remaining 1/4 cup caramel topping over pie. Cover and refrigerate any remaining pie.

High Altitude (3500–6500 ft): No change.

1 Serving: Calories 500; Total Fat 31g (Saturated Fat 16g; Trans Fat 0g); Cholesterol 55mg; Sodium 400mg; Total Carbohydrate 51g (Dietary Fiber 1g) Exchanges: 3 1/2 Other Carbohydrate, 1 High-Fat Meat, 4 1/2 Fat Carbohydrate Choices: 3 1/2

Ruth-Anne O'Gorman | Kodiak, AK

Ruth-Anne O'Gorman lives on Kodiak Island with 1,000 Kodiak brown bears and 14,000 people. The closest metropolitan area is Anchorage— which is one hour away by plane or 20 hours by ferry and car. Ruth-Anne does most of her creative cooking on the weekend and served this recipe as a dessert on Sunday evening. She describes her job as "keeping the population of Kodiak Island as healthy as possible." Ruth-Anne travels to remote villages on the island in small single engine planes to deliver health care.

- 2 packages (8 oz each) cream cheese, softened
- ½ cup creamy peanut butter
- 2 tablespoons honey
- 1 cup powdered sugar
- 1 roll (16.5 oz) Pillsbury refrigerated peanut butter cookies
- ¾ to 1 cup honey-roasted dry-roasted peanuts, coarsely chopped

jumbo honey-roasted peanut butter sandwich cookies

8 sandwich cookies | Prep Time: **25 minutes** | Start to Finish: **1 hour 10 minutes**

1 In large bowl, beat cream cheese, peanut butter and honey with electric mixer on medium speed until smooth. Add powdered sugar; beat just until smooth. Cover; refrigerate at least 1 hour while baking and cooling cookies.

2 Heat oven to 350°F. Make cookies as directed on package. Cool completely.

3 Spread ⅓ cup cream cheese mixture on bottom of 1 cookie; top with another cookie, bottom side down. Press cookies together slightly so cream cheese mixture extends just past edges of cookies. Roll edge of cream cheese mixture in chopped peanuts to generously coat. Repeat with remaining cookies.

4 Serve immediately, or store in single layer tightly covered in refrigerator up to 4 hours (cookies stored longer become very soft).

High Altitude (3500–6500 ft): No change.

1 Sandwich Cookie: Calories 730; Total Fat 47g (Saturated Fat 18g; Trans Fat 3g); Cholesterol 70mg; Sodium 560mg; Total Carbohydrate 60g (Dietary Fiber 2g) **Exchanges:** 1 Starch, 3 Other Carbohydrate, 2 High-Fat Meat, 6 Fat Carbohydrate Choices: 4

Karry Edwards | Sandy, UT

According to **Karry Edwards**, when people see and taste these rich, decadent cookies, "they cannot believe how simple they are to make." She says they can stand on their own as a special dessert. Karry calls herself a baker first, and then a cook. A favorite childhood photo pictures Karry and her brother in the kitchen, grinning proudly in front of the gingerbread cake she just baked. After learning she was a Bake-Off® Contest finalist, this mother says, "I floated home on a cloud."

1 box (12.8 oz) Cinnamon Toast Crunch® cereal (about 8 cups)

½ cup butter or margarine, melted

1 tablespoon corn syrup

1 box (19.5 oz) Pillsbury traditional fudge brownie mix

½ cup vegetable oil

¼ cup water

2 eggs

½ teaspoon ground cinnamon

1⅓ cups semisweet chocolate chips

3 tablespoons cinnamon-sugar (from 3.62-oz jar)*

Valerie Schucht | Glastonbury, CT

Experimental baking is **Valerie Schucht**'s specialty. In her quest to find the best—such as the best oatmeal cookie, best yellow cake or best blondie—she experiments with dozens of recipes. Her favorite ingredient? Butter. "You can't be a serious baker without having a lot of butter around!" says Valerie. As a teenager, she liked to flip through her mom's 1959 Best of the Bake-Off® Collection cookbook. "I would drool over the pictures and then decide on a recipe to make."

mexican chocolate crunch brownies

24 brownies | Prep Time: **20 minutes** | Start to Finish: **3 hours**

1 Heat oven to 350°F. Spray 13×9-inch pan with cooking spray. Place cereal in food processor bowl with metal blade (crush cereal in 2 batches if necessary). Cover; process until finely crushed (about 4 cups). Or place cereal in large resealable food-storage plastic bag; crush with rolling pin.

2 In large bowl, stir butter and corn syrup until well blended. Add crushed cereal; mix thoroughly. Press evenly in pan.

3 In large bowl, make brownie mix as directed on box, using oil, water and eggs and adding cinnamon. Stir in ⅔ cup of the chocolate chips. Pour brownie batter over cereal mixture. Sprinkle remaining ⅔ cup chocolate chips evenly over batter.

4 Bake 20 minutes. Sprinkle cinnamon-sugar evenly over brownies. Bake 14 to 18 minutes longer or until brownies are set when lightly touched in center. Cool 10 minutes; loosen edges but do not cut. Cool completely, about 2 hours. For brownies, cut into 6 rows by 4 rows.

*3 tablespoons sugar mixed with ½ teaspoon ground cinnamon can be substituted for the cinnamon-sugar.

High Altitude (3500–6500 ft): In step 2, after pressing cereal mixture evenly in pan, bake 5 to 8 minutes. Make brownie mix following High Altitude directions on box; pour over partially-baked crust.

1 Brownie: Calories 280; Total Fat 15g (Saturated Fat 5g; Trans Fat 0g); Cholesterol 25mg; Sodium 190mg; Total Carbohydrate 35g (Dietary Fiber 1g) Exchanges: ½ Starch, 1½ Other Carbohydrate, 3 Fat Carbohydrate Choices: 2

2 1/2 cups very finely chopped walnuts

6 tablespoons sugar

6 tablespoons butter or margarine, melted

1 roll (16.5 oz) Pillsbury refrigerated sugar cookies

1 tablespoon instant espresso coffee granules

1 1/2 cups dark chocolate chips

1/4 cup plus 2 tablespoons whipping cream

mocha-walnut bars with dark chocolate ganache

24 bars I Prep Time: **30 minutes** I Start to Finish: **3 hours 10 minutes**

1 Heat oven to 350°F. In medium bowl, stir walnuts, sugar and butter until moistened. Press mixture evenly on bottom of ungreased 13×9-inch pan or 12×8-inch (2-quart) glass baking dish. Bake 8 to 15 minutes or until edges are just golden brown. Cool 30 minutes.

2 In large bowl, knead cookie dough and espresso granules until blended. Drop small spoonfuls of dough evenly over walnut crust. Gently press dough together evenly over crust. (If dough is sticky, use floured fingers.)

3 Bake 20 to 25 minutes or until golden brown. Cool 30 minutes.

4 In medium microwavable bowl, microwave chocolate chips and whipping cream uncovered on High 1 minute, stirring after 30 seconds; stir until chips are melted and mixture is smooth. Spread chocolate mixture evenly over bars. Refrigerate 1 hour. For bars, cut into 6 rows by 4 rows. Cover and refrigerate any remaining bars.

High Altitude (3500–6500 ft): No change.

1 **Bar:** Calories 290; Total Fat 20g (Saturated Fat 6g; Trans Fat 1g); Cholesterol 20mg; Sodium 85mg; Total Carbohydrate 24g (Dietary Fiber 1g) **Exchanges:** 1 1/2 Other Carbohydrate, 1/2 High-Fat Meat, 3 Fat **Carbohydrate Choices:** 1 1/2

Elizabeth Bennett I **Mill Creek, WA**

According to **Elizabeth Bennett**, the hardest part about entering the Bake-Off® Contest was "I don't like to measure." Fortunately, she managed to pin down this recipe, inspired by her favorite candy: a caramel walnut square with dark chocolate. She added espresso to her recipe because, she explains, "As a true Seattleite, I just can't get enough coffee any time of day." Elizabeth launched her own event-planning business and enjoys seeing new parts of the world. In 2004, she traveled to Italy with two college girlfriends.

1 roll (16.5 oz) Pillsbury refrigerated sugar cookies
⅓ cup dry-roasted peanuts
⅓ cup caramel topping
¼ cup creamy peanut butter
½ teaspoon ground cinnamon
½ cup peanut butter chips
¼ cup white vanilla baking chips

nutty caramel cookie tart

16 servings | Prep Time: **20 minutes** | Start to Finish: **2 hours 5 minutes**

1 Heat oven to 350°F. Press cookie dough evenly in bottom of ungreased 9-inch springform pan. (If dough is sticky, use floured fingers.) Bake 17 to 22 minutes or until light golden brown.

2 Meanwhile, place peanuts in resealable food-storage plastic bag; seal bag. Crush peanuts with rolling pin or meat mallet; set aside.

3 In medium microwavable bowl, microwave caramel topping, peanut butter and cinnamon uncovered on High 30 to 60 seconds or until hot and bubbly; stir well. Drizzle mixture evenly over partially baked crust. Sprinkle evenly with peanut butter chips, vanilla baking chips and crushed peanuts.

4 Bake 12 to 18 minutes longer or until edges are golden brown. Cool completely, about 1 hour 30 minutes.

5 Run sharp knife carefully around edge of tart to loosen; remove side of pan. To serve, cut tart into wedges. Store tightly covered at room temperature.

High Altitude (3500–6500 ft): No change.

1 **Serving:** Calories 240; Total Fat 12g (Saturated Fat 3g; Trans Fat 2g); Cholesterol 10mg; Sodium 180mg; Total Carbohydrate 29g (Dietary Fiber 0g) **Exchanges:** 1 Starch, 1 Other Carbohydrate, 2 Fat **Carbohydrate Choices:** 2

Shannon Kohn | **Simpsonville, SC**

Shannon Kohn enjoys opening up the pantry and fridge to see the ingredients on hand and then thinking of creative, tasty ways to combine them. Shannon served this tart at a neighborhood Bunko party and "the ladies loved it." She concocts her creations in the kitchen of her dreams, which is part of a new house they built and moved into in 2006. Shannon describes herself as a "quick and easy" cook. "If a recipe is too long or complicated, I'll scrap the recipe and find another," she says.

1 roll (16.5 oz) Pillsbury refrigerated sugar
  cookies
1 bag (12 oz) semisweet chocolate chips
  (2 cups)
3 cups chopped pecans
1/2 cup butter or margarine
1/2 cup packed light brown sugar
1 jar (12.25 oz) caramel topping
1 cup graham cracker crumbs (16 squares)

ooey-gooey turtle bars

24 bars | Prep Time: **20 minutes** | Start to Finish: **4 hours 25 minutes**

1 Heat oven to 350°F (325°F for dark or nonstick pan). Press cookie dough evenly in bottom of ungreased 13×9-inch pan.

2 Sprinkle 1 cup of the chocolate chips and 1 1/2 cups of the pecans evenly over dough; lightly press into dough. Set aside.

3 In 2-quart saucepan, melt butter over medium-high heat. Stir in brown sugar, caramel topping and graham cracker crumbs. Heat to boiling, stirring constantly. Pour over crust in pan; spread evenly. Sprinkle evenly with remaining 1 cup chocolate chips and 1 1/2 cups pecans.

4 Bake 25 to 32 minutes or until edges are deep golden brown and pecans are lightly toasted. Cool on cooling rack 30 minutes; loosen sides from pan, but do not cut. Cool completely, about 3 hours longer. (For firmer bars, let stand an additional 2 hours.) For bars, cut into 6 rows by 4 rows.

High Altitude (3500–6500 ft): Bake 27 to 34 minutes.

1 Bar: Calories 370; Total Fat 22g (Saturated Fat 7g; Trans Fat 2g); Cholesterol 15mg; Sodium 160mg; Total Carbohydrate 40g (Dietary Fiber 2g) **Exchanges:** 1 Starch, 1 1/2 Other Carbohydrate, 4 1/2 Fat **Carbohydrate Choices:** 2 1/2

Gretchen Wanek | Oshkosh, WI

After perfecting her recipe, **Gretchen Wanek** served it to her family, who asked her to make it again and again. Gretchen whipped up a batch for her husband to take to work. "He told me the guys couldn't stop raving about them." The co-workers who didn't get any begged him to bring more the next day, she says. Gretchen says her recipe is easy to follow, hard to "flub" and "so addicting that they don't last long and you have to make more." Her cooking specialty is home-made egg rolls.

Ingredients

1 roll (16.5 oz) Pillsbury refrigerated sugar cookies

2 tablespoons grated orange peel (from 2 large oranges)

2 packages (8 oz each) cream cheese, softened

1/4 cup sugar

1/2 cup orange marmalade

1 teaspoon orange-flavored liqueur or 1/4 teaspoon orange extract

2 eggs

3 tablespoons whipping cream

2 drops orange food color (or 2 drops yellow and 1 drop red food color)

1 1/2 teaspoons butter or margarine

1/2 cup white vanilla baking chips

orange cream dessert squares

24 servings | Prep Time: **25 minutes** | Start to Finish: **3 hours 35 minutes**

1 Heat oven to 350°F. Press cookie dough evenly on bottom and 1 inch up sides of ungreased 13×9-inch (3-quart) glass baking dish. (If dough is sticky, use floured fingers.) Sprinkle evenly with orange peel.

2 In medium bowl, beat cream cheese, sugar, marmalade and liqueur with electric mixer on medium-high speed about 1 minute or until well blended. Add eggs; beat about 2 minutes or until well blended and mixture is creamy. Spread evenly in crust.

3 Bake 29 to 36 minutes or until crust is golden brown and center is set. Cool 1 hour.

4 In small microwavable bowl, microwave whipping cream and food color uncovered on High about 30 seconds or just until boiling. Add butter and baking chips; stir until chips are melted. Spread mixture evenly over bars. Refrigerate about 1 1/2 hours or until chilled and firm.

5 For squares, cut into 6 rows by 4 rows, using thin, sharp knife and wiping blade occasionally. Cover and refrigerate any remaining dessert squares.

High Altitude (3500-6500 ft): No change.

1 Serving: Calories 210; Total Fat 13g (Saturated Fat 6g; Trans Fat 1g); Cholesterol 45mg; Sodium 135mg; Total Carbohydrate 22g (Dietary Fiber 0g) Exchanges: 1/2 Starch, 1 Other Carbohydrate, 2 1/2 Fat Carbohydrate Choices: 1 1/2

Bonny Boyd | Dubuque, IA

Bonny Boyd says her Bake-Off® recipe "brings back memories of a childhood treat." It has an orange marmalade-cream cheese filling that reminds her of a Dreamsicle. The rich bars are so simple to make that it's hard to go wrong, she says. Bonny also is known for her pie prowess. She says, "I think my husband married me for my apple pie." Bonny's home was built in the 1880s. Everything in the small kitchen is original, except the appliances, she says. A self-described country cook, Bonny likes cooking hearty food with good ingredients.

1 box (13.3 oz) Pillsbury peanut butter swirl brownie mix

2 cups crushed chocolate or regular graham crackers (28 squares)

1/2 cup plus 3 tablespoons butter or margarine

1 can (14 oz) sweetened condensed milk (not evaporated)

1/3 cup creamy peanut butter

1 1/4 cups peanut butter chips

3/4 cup milk chocolate chips

1 cup Spanish peanuts, finely chopped

Sheilah Fiola | Kent, WA

Sheilah Fiola remembers her family's laughter when she served them partially frozen Brussels sprouts. Her cooking has come a long way since then and no one's laughing now. In fact, Sheila's Italian entrées are so good that her husband no longer likes dining out at Italian restaurants. Sheilah learned to cook by watching her mother and her Aunt Mildred. She combined peanut butter brownie mix, peanut butter, peanut butter chips and peanuts to create this treat that she says is great for gatherings and tailgate parties.

peanuttiest peanut butter brownie bars

24 bars | Prep Time: **30 minutes** | Start to Finish: **3 hours 55 minutes**

1 Heat oven to 350°F. Lightly spray 13×9-inch pan with cooking spray.

2 In large bowl, stir dry brownie mix and graham cracker crumbs until well mixed; set aside.

3 Into medium microwavable bowl, squeeze peanut butter from peanut butter packet (from brownie mix). Add butter. Microwave uncovered on High 1 minute to 1 minute 30 seconds, stirring once, until butter is melted. Stir until smooth.

4 Pour peanut butter mixture over brownie mixture; stir until well mixed. Press evenly in pan.

5 In same medium microwavable bowl, mix milk, 1/3 cup peanut butter and 1/2 cup of the peanut butter chips. Microwave uncovered on High 1 minute, stirring once, until mixture is melted. Stir until smooth.

6 Gently pour milk mixture evenly over brownie layer in pan; spread evenly. Sprinkle remaining 3/4 cup peanut butter chips, the chocolate chips and peanuts evenly over milk mixture; press in lightly.

7 Bake 18 to 22 minutes or until edges are golden brown and center is just set when lightly touched (do not overbake). Cool completely in pan on cooling rack, about 3 hours. For bars, cut into 6 rows by 4 rows.

High Altitude (3500-6500 ft): Bake 25 to 30 minutes.

1 Bar: Calories 350; Total Fat 20g (Saturated Fat 9g; Trans Fat 1g); Cholesterol 20mg; Sodium 190mg; Total Carbohydrate 35g (Dietary Fiber 1g) **Exchanges:** 1 Starch, 1 1/2 Other Carbohydrate, 1/2 High-Fat Meat, 3 Fat **Carbohydrate Choices:** 2

CAKE

1 box (19.5 oz) Pillsbury traditional fudge brownie mix

1/2 cup canola oil

1/4 cup water

3 eggs

MOUSSE

1 box (4-serving size) pistachio instant pudding and pie filling mix

3/4 cup cold whole milk

1 cup cold whipping cream

1/2 cup pistachio nuts, coarsely chopped

GLAZE

1/2 cup whipping cream

4 oz semisweet baking chocolate, finely chopped

1 teaspoon vanilla

1 teaspoon light corn syrup

GARNISH

1/2 cup whipping cream

2 tablespoons powdered sugar

Reserved 1 tablespoon pistachio instant pudding and pie filling mix

Jane Estrin | Gainesville, FL

As her son approached the end of high school, **Jane Estrin** had extra time. So she decided to dive deeper into her favorite pastime: cooking and baking, particularly desserts like this torte. The combination of chocolate and pistachio is delicious, she says. It's no wonder she loves Italian cooking: both of her parents' families are Italian. When Jane was young, her mother was ill on Thanksgiving. Jane cooked the entire meal, running between her mother's room for instructions and the kitchen.

pistachio mousse brownie torte

16 servings | Prep Time: **1 hour** | Start to Finish: **2 hours 45 minutes**

1 Heat oven to 350°F. Lightly spray bottom of 2 (8-inch) round cake pans with cooking spray. Line bottoms of pans with cooking parchment paper; lightly spray paper with cooking spray.

2 In large bowl, stir brownie mix, oil, water and eggs 50 strokes with spoon. Spread half of batter (1 1/2 cups) evenly in each pan.

3 Bake 27 to 30 minutes or until toothpick inserted 2 inches from edge of pan comes out clean. Cool in pans on cooling racks 10 minutes. Run knife around edge of pans to loosen. Place cooling rack upside down on 1 pan; turn rack and pan over. Remove pan and parchment paper. Repeat with second brownie layer. Place racks with brownie layers in refrigerator to cool completely, about 20 minutes.

4 Meanwhile, measure 1 tablespoon of the pudding mix; reserve for garnish. In large bowl, beat remaining pudding mix, the milk and 1 cup whipping cream with electric mixer on high speed about 2 minutes or until mixture is thick and creamy. Stir in nuts. Cover; refrigerate.

5 Carefully cut each brownie layer horizontally in half, using long serrated knife, to make 4 layers. On serving plate, place 1 brownie layer, cut side down. Spread 1/3 of the mousse (3/4 cup) evenly to edge of brownie. Repeat layering twice, using 2 brownie layers (place cut sides down) and remaining mousse. Top with remaining brownie layer, cut side down. Refrigerate torte while making glaze.

6 In 1-quart saucepan, heat 1/2 cup whipping cream over medium heat, stirring occasionally, just until bubbles start to form at edge of saucepan. Remove from heat. Add chocolate; stir constantly until smooth. Stir in vanilla and corn syrup; let stand 10 minutes. Stir glaze; spoon over top of torte, allowing some to run down side. Return torte to refrigerator while making garnish.

7   In medium bowl, beat ½ cup whipping cream, the powdered sugar and reserved 1 tablespoon pudding mix on high speed until stiff peaks form. Spoon mixture into decorating bag fitted with star tip and pipe rosettes on top of torte, or spoon dollops of mixture on torte. Refrigerate at least 30 minutes before serving. Cover and refrigerate any remaining torte.

High Altitude (3500–6500 ft): For cake, increase water to ⅓ cup and add ½ cup all-purpose flour.

1 Serving: Calories 380; Total Fat 25g (Saturated Fat 9g; Trans Fat 0g); Cholesterol 70mg; Sodium 200mg; Total Carbohydrate 34g (Dietary Fiber 1g) **Exchanges:** 1 Starch, 1 Other Carbohydrate, 5 Fat **Carbohydrate Choices:** 2

1 box (15.5 oz) Pillsbury chocolate chunk
   brownie mix
1/4 cup Pillsbury BEST all-purpose flour
1/2 cup butter or margarine, melted
1 egg
1 teaspoon vanilla
1/4 cup plus 2 tablespoons red raspberry
   preserves
2 to 4 teaspoons powdered sugar
12 fresh raspberries, if desired

raspberry-filled brownie delights

12 sandwich cookies | Prep Time: **35 minutes** | Start to Finish: **1 hour
20 minutes**

1 Heat oven to 375°F. In large bowl, stir together brownie mix and flour. Add butter, egg and vanilla; stir until blended. Let dough stand 15 minutes for easier handling.

2 Shape dough into 24 (about 1 1/2-inch) balls (dough will be soft). Place 2 inches apart on ungreased large cookie sheet.

3 Bake 10 to 13 minutes or until set and tops appear dry. Cool on cookie sheet 1 minute; remove from cookie sheet to cooling rack. Cool completely, about 30 minutes.

4 Spread 1 1/2 teaspoons preserves on bottom of 1 cookie; top with another cookie, bottom side down. Repeat with remaining cookies. Sprinkle powdered sugar through fine-mesh strainer or sieve over cookies. Place on serving platter; top each cookie with raspberry.

High Altitude (3500–6500 ft): Heat oven to 350°F. Decrease butter to 1/3 cup.

1 Sandwich Cookie: Calories 280; Total Fat 13g (Saturated Fat 7g; Trans Fat 1g); Cholesterol 35mg; Sodium 105mg; Total Carbohydrate 39g (Dietary Fiber 0g) **Exchanges:** 1/2 Starch, 2 Other Carbohydrate, 2 1/2 Fat **Carbohydrate Choices:** 2 1/2

Teresa Ralston | New Albany, OH

Teresa Ralston's recipe features the classic combination of chocolate and raspberry. It looks and tastes spectacular, she says. Teresa first made the recipe when her kids were at school and served it as an after-school snack. They said, "Mom, that's a winner!" To encourage creativity and a love of cooking and baking, Teresa's children have their own cookbooks, cooking utensils and baking supplies stocked on low kitchen shelves. "I absolutely love to bake in the kitchen with my kids," she says. "There is so much to be gained cooking, learning and spending quality time in the kitchen. It's truly a passion for me."

TORTE

1 can (8 oz) or 1 package (7 oz) almond
    paste
3 tablespoons butter or margarine, softened
1 egg white
3 oz semisweet baking chocolate, melted
1 Pillsbury refrigerated pie crust (from 15-oz
    box), softened as directed on box
2 tablespoons seedless red raspberry jam
1/4 cup sliced almonds

GARNISHES

1 teaspoon powdered sugar
1 cup whipped cream

Lori Welander | Richmond, VA

Chocolate is the favorite
ingredient of everyone
Lori Welander bakes for,
especially her husband
and son. So it makes
sense that chocolate
appears in her Bake-Off® entry, which
also reflects elements from fruit cro-
stadas and almond frangipane tortes.
When a hurricane hit Richmond in
2003, Lori's entire neighborhood was
without power. Neighbors pooled all
their perishable food, and Lori coordi-
nated recipes, preparation and grilling
for a huge block party. An annual
neighborhood party continues today.

raspberry-kissed chocolate-almond crostada

8 servings | Prep Time: **20 minutes** | Start to Finish: **2 hours**

1 Heat oven to 375°F. Spray large cookie sheet with cooking spray, or line with cooking parchment paper.

2 Break up almond paste into medium bowl; add butter and egg white. Beat with electric mixer on medium speed until smooth. Beat in melted chocolate until well blended. (Or, in food processor bowl with metal blade, break up almond paste; add butter and egg white. Cover; process with on-and-off pulses until smooth. Add melted chocolate. Cover; process until smooth.)

3 Unroll pie crust; place on center of cookie sheet. Spoon almond filling onto middle of crust; spread evenly to within 1 1/2 to 2 inches of edge. Fold edge of crust over filling, forming pleats; press down slightly. Spread jam evenly over filling. Sprinkle almonds over filling and crust.

4 Bake 25 to 35 minutes or until crust is golden brown. Cool com-pletely, about 1 hour. Garnish top with light sprinkling of pow-dered sugar and dollops of whipped cream.

High Altitude (3500–6500 ft): No change.

1 **Serving:** Calories 430; Total Fat 28g (Saturated Fat 11g; Trans Fat 0g); Cholesterol 30mg; Sodium 160mg; Total Car-bohydrate 40g (Dietary Fiber 2g) **Exchanges:** 1 1/2 Starch, 1 Other Carbohydrate, 5 1/2 Fat **Carbohydrate Choices:** 2 1/2

1 roll (16.5 oz) Pillsbury refrigerated chocolate chip cookies

2 packages (8 oz each) cream cheese, softened

1 jar (12.25 oz) caramel topping

$1/2$ cup creamy peanut butter

$1/3$ cup powdered sugar

1 teaspoon vanilla

$1/4$ teaspoon ground cinnamon

$1/8$ teaspoon freshly grated nutmeg or regular ground nutmeg

1 container (8 oz) frozen whipped topping, thawed

$1^1/_4$ cups honey-roasted peanuts

spiced creamy caramel-peanut torte

16 servings | Prep Time: **20 minutes** | Start to Finish: **1 hour 55 minutes**

1 Heat oven to 350°F. Spray 10- or 9-inch springform pan with cooking spray. Press cookie dough on bottom and $1/4$ inch up side of pan. Bake 16 to 23 minutes or until golden brown. Cool completely, about 45 minutes.

2 Meanwhile, in large bowl, beat cream cheese, $2/3$ cup of the caramel topping, the peanut butter and powdered sugar with electric mixer on medium speed until smooth. Beat in vanilla, cinnamon and nutmeg. Fold in whipped topping until well mixed. Fold in 1 cup of the peanuts. Cover; refrigerate until crust is completely cooled.

3 Spoon cream cheese mixture evenly over cookie crust. Freeze at least 30 minutes until set.

4 Just before serving, top torte with remaining $1/4$ cup peanuts and drizzle with remaining $1/3$ cup caramel topping. For easier cutting, wipe knife after each cut. Cover and refrigerate any remaining torte.

High Altitude (3500–6500 ft): No change.

1 Serving: Calories 460; Total Fat 28g (Saturated Fat 12g; Trans Fat 2g); Cholesterol 35mg; Sodium 330mg; Total Carbohydrate 43g (Dietary Fiber 2g) **Exchanges:** 1 Starch, 2 Other Carbohydrate, 1 High-Fat Meat, $3^1/_2$ Fat **Carbohydrate Choices:** 3

Jennifer Howeth | **Newcastle, OK**

"Desserts just make people happy," says **Jennifer Howeth**. That's one reason they're her favorite thing to make. This torte starts with a chocolate chip cookie crust. Jennifer says it has a creamy, nutty, caramel richness that has people reaching for a second piece. When Jennifer was young, her mother asked her to blanch a bushel of fresh corn. Imagine her mother's surprise when she found a bathtub full of hot water and corn! If Jennifer had won the grand prize money, she would have installed a pool and taken a fabulous vacation.

1 box (19.5 oz) Pillsbury traditional fudge brownie mix
1/2 cup vegetable oil
1/4 cup water
3 eggs
1 1/2 cups toffee bits
1 cup macadamia nuts, chopped
2 firm ripe medium bananas, cut into 1/4-inch pieces (2 cups)
1/3 cup caramel topping

toffee-banana brownies

24 brownies | Prep Time: **20 minutes** | Start to Finish: **3 hours 10 minutes**

1 Heat oven to 350°F. Generously spray 13×9-inch pan with cooking spray.

2 In medium bowl, stir brownie mix, oil, water and eggs 50 strokes with spoon. Add 1 cup of the toffee bits, the nuts and bananas; stir just until well blended. Pour into pan. Sprinkle remaining 1/2 cup toffee bits evenly over top.

3 Bake 38 to 48 minutes or until center is set when lightly touched, top is slightly dry and edges just start to pull away from sides of pan. Cool completely, about 2 hours. For brownies, cut into 6 rows by 4 rows. To serve, drizzle each brownie with caramel topping. Cover and refrigerate any remaining brownies.

High Altitude (3500–6500 ft): Increase water to 1/3 cup. Add 1/2 cup all-purpose flour to dry brownie mix.

1 Brownie: Calories 260; Total Fat 15g (Saturated Fat 3g; Trans Fat 0g); Cholesterol 105mg; Sodium 75mg; Total Carbohydrate 30g (Dietary Fiber 0g) **Exchanges:** 1/2 Starch, 1 1/2 Other Carbohydrate, 3 Fat **Carbohydrate Choices:** 2

Gwen Beauchamp | Lancaster, TX

A confirmed chocoholic with a husband who loves brownies, **Gwen Beauchamp** decided to reinvent a favorite brownie recipe. "Chocolate still rules," says Gwen, "it just has some new friends." They're rich new friends too: macadamia nuts, toffee bits, diced banana and caramel. "You don't get much simpler than putting all the ingredients in one bowl and stirring with a spoon, then pouring it in the pan," she says. Gwen's response to learning she was a Bake-Off® Contest finalist? "Disbelief! Excitement! Surprise! Shock!"

1 box (19.5 oz) Pillsbury milk chocolate
   brownie mix
1/2 cup canola oil
1/4 cup water
4 eggs
1 package (8 oz) cream cheese, softened
1 cup seedless red raspberry jam
1/4 cup sour cream
1 teaspoon vanilla
1 jar (11.75 oz) hot fudge topping
1/2 cup fresh red raspberries
Fresh mint sprigs
1 quart vanilla ice cream, if desired

Karen Bowlden | Boise, ID

Karen Bowlden learned
how to cook from her
mom, who had nine
mouths to feed. "My
mom is the best cook
in the world," she says.
"Off-the-charts desserts and cakes"
are Karen's specialties. She describes
this pudding cake as "pure comfort
food" because it's tasty, warm and
gooey. Karen's dad met her Korean
mom in Pearl Harbor during the war.
Their family still celebrates Korean
food traditions, including a traditional
meal with tender beef slices dipped in
egg batter and then pan-fried. Karen's
favorite meal is her mom's Korean
bulgogi.

warm and fudgy raspberry pudding cake

12 servings | Prep Time: **20 minutes** | Start to Finish: **1 hour 40 minutes**

1 Heat oven to 350°F. Spray 13×9-inch (3-quart) glass baking dish
with cooking spray.

2 In large bowl, stir brownie mix, oil, water and 2 of the eggs 50 strokes
with spoon. Pour into baking dish.

3 In medium bowl, beat cream cheese and jam with electric mixer on
medium speed until well mixed. Beat in remaining 2 eggs, the sour
cream and vanilla until well mixed (mixture will be runny). Pour
over brownie batter. Swirl mixtures slightly with a spoon or tip of
knife for marbled design.

4 Bake 35 to 50 minutes or until edges are golden brown and center
is puffed and set when lightly touched.

5 Warm jar of fudge topping as directed on label. Pour evenly over
cake, spreading to cover if necessary. Cool 30 to 45 minutes before
serving. Garnish with raspberries and mint sprigs. Serve with ice
cream.

High Altitude (3500–6500 ft): Make brownies following High Altitude package directions. Bake 40 to 50 minutes.

1 Serving: Calories 540; Total Fat 24g (Saturated Fat 7g; Trans Fat 0g); Cholesterol 85mg; Sodium 300mg; Total
Carbohydrate 74g (Dietary Fiber 1g) Exchanges: 1 Starch, 4 Other Carbohydrate, 1/2 Medium-Fat Meat, 4 Fat Carbohydrate Choices: 5

metric conversion guide

VOLUME

U.S. Units	Canadian Metric	Australian Metric
1/4 teaspoon	1 mL	1 ml
1/2 teaspoon	2 mL	2 ml
1 teaspoon	5 mL	5 ml
1 tablespoon	15 mL	20 ml
1/4 cup	50 mL	60 ml
1/3 cup	75 mL	80 ml
1/2 cup	125 mL	125 ml
2/3 cup	150 mL	170 ml
3/4 cup	175 mL	190 ml
1 cup	250 mL	250 ml
1 quart	1 liter	1 liter
1 1/2 quarts	1.5 liters	1.5 liters
2 quarts	2 liters	2 liters
2 1/2 quarts	2.5 liters	2.5 liters
3 quarts	3 liters	3 liters
4 quarts	4 liters	4 liters

WEIGHT

U.S. Units	Canadian Metric	Australian Metric
1 ounce	30 grams	30 grams
2 ounces	55 grams	60 grams
3 ounces	85 grams	90 grams
4 ounces (1/4 pound)	115 grams	125 grams
8 ounces (1/2 pound)	225 grams	225 grams
16 ounces (1 pound)	455 grams	500 grams
1 pound	455 grams	0.5 kilogram

Note: The recipes in this cookbook have not been developed or tested using metric measures. When converting recipes to metric, some variations in quality may be noted.

MEASUREMENTS

Inches	Centimeters
1	2.5
2	5.0
3	7.5
4	10.0
5	12.5
6	15.0
7	17.5
8	20.5
9	23.0
10	25.5
11	28.0
12	30.5
13	33.0

TEMPERATURES

Fahrenheit	Celsius
32°	0°
212°	100°
250°	120°
275°	140°
300°	150°
325°	160°
350°	180°
375°	190°
400°	200°
425°	220°
450°	230°
475°	240°
500°	260°

index

Page numbers in *italics* indicate illustrations

RECIPES

CATEGORIES

* indicates category-winning recipe.

MEET THE FINALISTS

Alaska
O'Gorman, Ruth-Anne, 192

California
Chan, Roxanne, 106
Chittock, Sharon, 102
Connick, Wendy, 18
Dahlman, David, 52
Hickam, Linda, 180
Ko, Wendy, 54
McDonogh, Lana, 64
Morrison, Kathryn, 162
Pittman, Laureen, 48
Roper, Sherry, 120
Singer, Gail, 70
Weeks-Daniel, Phyllis, 9, 56

Colorado
Carpenter, Harrison, 166
Fluck, Kimberly, 100
Frantz, Kim, 176
Martinez, Margaret, 116

Connecticut
Schucht, Valerie, 196

Delaware
Corby, Jan, 82

Florida
Albert, Natalie, 58
Denny, Diane, 20
Estrin, Jane, 208
Harkleroad, Jennifer, 88
Hyde, Robin, 148
Johnston, Sherry, 154

Georgia
Puette, Deborah, 126
Tapia, Pamela, 108
Williams, Barbara, 164
Wright, Ayofemi, 184

Idaho
Bowlden, Karen, 218

Illinois
Johnson, Monika, 168
Riva, Annette, 96
Wara, Dianna, 92

Indiana
Felts, Gloria, 122
Klinedinst, Sherry, 62
Kramer, Lisa, 32
Rossell, Beverley, 190

Iowa
Boyd, Bonny, 204
Solt, Norita, 42

Maryland
Couch, Erika, 12
Gurtz, Carolyn, 9, 178, 186
Haller, Kathleen, 40

Massachusetts
Buliga, Jasmine, 90
Kerns, Tena, 118
Pando, Julie, 72
Plourde, Niki, 9, 142
Sinkevicius, Kerstin, 182

Michigan
Engelhart, Bee, 174

Minnesota
Naumann, Paula, 84
Rudberg, Edgar, 9, 50, 78

Missouri
Hahn, Barbara, 124
Strunk, Alison, 76

Montana
Gadsby, Bob, 158

New Hampshire
Brnger, Amy, 150

New Jersey
Colon, Patty, 44
Ingalls, Patricia, 66

New Mexico
Kalb, Patricia, 170
Moore, Melinda, 36

New York
Feldman, Vicki, 30
Pozzanghera, Vanda, 9, 94, 112
Schuhmacher, Tracy, 68

North Carolina
Blount, Margaret, 86

Ohio
Bibbo, Linda, 22
Gottfried, Jean, 26
Hukalo, Eva, 156
Koebel, Sharon, 134
Madyun, Audrey, 46
Ralston, Teresa, 210

Oklahoma
Howeth, Jennifer, 214
Reid, Sherrie, 152

Oregon
Sepich, Kathy, 146

Pennsylvania
Batton, Chris, 172
D'Amato, Theresa, 24
Hatfield, Scott, 80
Suhan, Sheila, 104

South Carolina
Gulkin, Karen, 128
Kohn, Shannon, 200

Tennessee
Bowser, Cynthia, 114
Lafon, Sarah, 136

Texas
Beauchamp, Gwen, 9, 216
Finley, Debbie, 144
Hill, Robin, 132
Hollowell, Stephanie, 188
Mandola, Mary Beth, 14
Pietsch, Frances, 110
Strachan, Carole, 140

Utah
Edwards, Karry, 194
Hilterbrand, DeAnn, 98

Virginia
Briggs, Mike, 130
Kompa, Noelle, 60
Welander, Lori, 212

Washington
Bennett, Elizabeth, 198
Fiola, Sheilah, 206

West Virginia
Shank, Pamela, 9, 10, 34
Smith, Sherry, 16
Sperry, Will, 28

Wisconsin
Benda, Laurie, 74
Heimerl, Renee, 38
Wanek, Gretchen, 202

Wyoming
Martinez, Tracy C., 160